Your Guide to MODELLING HERITAGE RAILWAYS
including railway centres & museums

I t is my pleasure, on behalf of the RAILWAY MODELLER team, to welcome you to *Modelling Heritage Railways*, another of the titles in the Peco Modellers' library which has been a real delight to put together. For me, especially so, since I have had the good fortune to follow the preservation movement as it grew from humble beginnings into the massive UK-wide leisure industry phenomenon that it is today.

My first ever visit to a preservation site took me to the Keighley & Worth Valley line in West Yorkshire in 1969. It was only some nine months since the line had been granted its light railway order and I was eager with excitement. Being truly honest though, I was a little disappointed, for the first preserved train in which I rode was nothing more than a small four-wheeled diesel railbus, something that to me as a 15 year old schoolboy seemed little different to the trains then commonplace on the main line. My disappointment was hopelessly misplaced however; those days were pioneering ones for all the preservation movements, and I was, no doubt, a little naïve to the tasks which the society and its dedicated volunteers then faced.

Fifty years on and things have changed beyond belief. Hundreds of societies, groups and private individuals have entered the arena, preservation projects pop up in places that you would never imagine, and there's an amazing inventory of rescued, rebuilt and refurbished stock to furnish services on all the reopened lines.

From a modelling point of view, heritage railways provide a great alternative to the far more common approach of replicating a company line, either historical or contemporary; or an industrial railway setting, narrow gauge or otherwise. Moreover, the restrictions associated with adherence to historical periods – as some schools of modelmaking dictate – are largely irrelevant. A heritage railway can readily embrace the railway scene across all eras without losing credibility: curious anachronisms with rolling stock actually become authentic in a way traditional historical railway modelling cannot justify.

That's not to imply that anything goes, as many lines like to operate speciality days, such as all-steam events, or diesel-only galas, some even run freight-only specials for photographers. In model form, your layout based on a preserved line thus becomes several layouts in one; steam one day, diesel another, goods only another, and so on.

In all the popular scales, even 7mm O gauge, there is huge scope amongst the ready-to-run models available for tackling a heritage line. It is steadily becoming the topic of choice for many modellers, young and old, and if you still want to include some 'proper' railway activity, a joint layout incorporating both is a valid concept, with genuine examples of such practices being the Preston Docks line or the stretch of Network Rail's tracks between Grosmont and Whitby.

Even in a book as comprehensive as this one, we cannot possibly hope to cover all the heritage railways that exist in Britain today. We have however included a wonderful selection of differing layout themes and schemes from which you can build a layout directly, or take as inspiration towards a plan of your own.

The UK is the birthplace of railways, and as a nation we are blessed with a truly unique and varied collection of railwayana from which tens of thousands gain enjoyment and advance their knowledge every year. That heritage provides a fantastic reserve of inspiration and wonder, enviable the world over, and one which we can experience and research first hand: ideal in fact for gathering all the information we might need for our next exciting layout project.

Steve Flint
Editor

Below
Trevor Powell's preservation-era scene *Rainford Stoops.*

Editor & Photographer
Steve Flint

Production Editor
Tim Rayner

Features Writer & Photographer
Craig Tiley

Editorial Assistant
Julie Newbery

Art Director
Adrian Stickland

Additional Photography
Derek Shore, Len Weal.
All uncredited photography by
Craig Tiley

Graphic Illustration
Dave Clements, Gary Bickley,
Steve Croucher

Peco Modelmakers
David Malton, Andrew Beard and
Ian Thompson

General & Advertisement Manager
John King

Advertisement Assistants
Sue Davis and Nicole Charlton

Direct Subscriptions
Alicia Knight

Chairman
C M Pritchard

Editorial Office Telephone
01297 20580

ISBN 978-0-900586-59-0

Contents

62

12

24

84

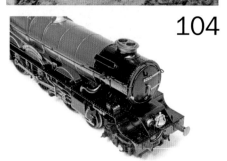

104

12 Chapter 1: **History of railway preservation in the UK**
We trace the lineage of railway preservation, not only from the post-WW2 enthusiast revivals such as
the Talyllyn and Bluebell railways, but back to the dawn of steam locomotion itself.

24 Chapter 2: **Standard gauge heritage railways**
These lines form the backbone of the preservation scene, and a selection of prototypes is offered as
well as some layouts that have been inspired by this branch of the heritage railway movement.

62 Chapter 3: **Railway centres and museums**
These are more compact preservation sites, some of which have been relocated from their initial
bases; they offer a focal point for a layout representing a longer line, or main line interface.

84 Chapter 4: **Narrow gauge and miniature railways**
Not only does the preservation movement owe much to the pioneering narrow gauge revivals of the
1950s, but many modern schemes involve the rebirth of standard gauge trackbeds as NG railways.

104 Chapter 5: **Modelling the preservation scene**
Individual projects to inspire you such as the creation of a locomotive as running in preservation; a
scrapyard restoration-in-waiting; and old coaches as volunteer accommodation, and more.

The appeal of modelling heritage railways

Traditionally, the majority of model railways that are featured in the pages of RAILWAY MODELLER or displayed at exhibitions are either historic depictions of a particular era (such as pre-Grouping steam or post-TOPS BR blue), or contemporary renditions of the national network. Such layouts have long proven popular, but what if

you are a modeller with a collection of locomotives and stock spanning multiple eras or regions, and therefore choosing a particular location or time period is proving difficult? Or maybe you have a particular liking for steam locomotives in pre-Grouping liveries, but feel daunted by the prospect of researching for a layout set prior to 1923? Perhaps you would just like to run your favourite models how and when you like, in a mixed environment? If you find yourself grappling with any such dilemmas, then why not consider a preservation scheme as the basis for your project?

Land of opportunity

Great Britain boasts a rich tapestry of preserved railways, heritage centres and working museums that have established themselves throughout the decades since the 1950s. Such localities occupy former

Left
Former branch and secondary routes account for the majority of standard gauge heritage lines. This is Goathland (on the North Yorkshire Moors Railway), which has been replicated in model form a number of times.

Below
Simon and Hannah Denham used Hornby Skaledale resin buildings on their OO gauge preservation-era portrayal of Goathland, which features models of locomotives from the NYMR fleet.
Photo: Steve Flint

Left
A section of the former Great Central Railway main line is preserved, much of it with double track operation – a unique feature on a UK preserved railway. In a scene that typifies the preservation era, repatriated WD 2-8-0 No.90733 (a pseudo BR identity) heads south with a passenger working, composed of an LMS-liveried inspection saloon and BR Southern Region stock.

Below left
GWR broad gauge operations have been resurrected at the Didcot Railway Centre with replica locomotives and stock, running for a short distance parallel to the centre's standard gauge demonstration branch line, thereby presenting opportunities to juxtapose locomotives and stock from different eras side by side.

Below
The Tanfield Railway in County Durham operates along parts of a former colliery system. The railway is home to a wide variety of industrial locomotives, with passenger trains composed of coaches with bodies fabricated from scratch atop four-wheel chassis. *Photo: Phil Barnes*

branch routes and main lines, locomotive depots and industrial networks, and cover standard, narrow – and even broad – gauges.

The heritage railway movement in the UK proliferated during the late 1960s – the catalyst being the sudden wideps-read closures of rail routes across the national network that occured as a result of Dr Beeching's infamous report, pub-lished in 1963. The violent eradication – seemingly overnight – of hundreds of stations and thousands of miles of rail routes spawned numerous groups of enthusiasts across the country to save and preserve the railway history that was fast being swept away.

A large number of the embryonic schemes that were founded during this period sought purely to restore stations and sections of abandoned railway routes to their pre-closure conditions, aspiring to become veritable time capsules of a lost era of rail travel behind steam locomotion. However, the ensuing decades have seen heritage railways evolve consider-ably, growing to become significant players in the country's multi-million pound tourism industry and writing their own histories in the process.

Many of the larger heritage railways that thrive today boast operations and financial turnovers that far exceed the aspirations of their original founders.

Bottom left
David and Robert Waller chose to model Ddaullt on the Festiniog Railway, set in the late 1980s and modelled in 009. The narrow gauge spiral track formation replicates the preservation-era deviation constructed by the reborn FR during its efforts to re-open the route back through to Blaneau Festiniog. *Photo: Len Weal*

Left
The restored Welshpool & Llanfair Railway is home to two original WLLR Beyer Peacock locomotives. However, prior to the delivery of replica coaching stock based on the railway's original designs, passenger trains utilised a selection of overseas-outline stock from Austria and Hungary.

Above
Recorded on 4 April 1976, this evocative scene exemplifies how a preservation theme for a layout can be placed in an historical context; a pair of Austerity 0-6-0STs depart Keighley on the then-fledgling Worth Valley line, with numerous Electricity Board vans providing tantalising period foreground interest.
Photo: Colour Rail

All things old and new

This evolution has included heritage schemes developing infrastructure to suit the specific needs that their preservation era operations demand, whether this be constructing brand new stations, bridges or dedicated locomotive restoration facilities, providing covered accommodation for vintage coaching stock or introducing state-of-the-art catering and visitor facilities. However, as a result of modern building regulations and financial considerations, many such infrastructure projects have often been completed in a modern style that contrasts with the original structures and artefacts with which they are integrated.

Such juxtapositions of old and new are particularly evident with collections of preserved locomotives and rolling stock; redundant main line vehicles are added continuously to heritage railway collections, which means that many railways have become homes to an eclectic mix of vehicles from different eras; steam locomotives in pre-Grouping liveries sharing duties with TOPS-numbered diesel locomotives in BR blue livery, or perhaps Victorian four-wheel carriages conveying passengers alongside BR Mk.II stock, and examples of unfitted wagons sharing siding space with air-braked freight stock and plant machinery.

Furthermore, the contrast of old and new is not just con-

Right
The Gloucestershire Warwickshire Steam Railway is typical of many operations that established a headquarters at a station where originally there were no locomotive servicing facilities. Therefore new infrastructure had to be constructed to suit the needs of operating a steam railway. This is part of the modern running shed and workshop complex at Toddington.

Right
Oliver Reading exploited the visual contrast of modern architecture and heritage traction on his fictional N gauge preservation scheme, *The Sheaf Valley Railway*. The workshops were constructed using brick paper for the base walls and embossed styrene sheet to represent the steel upper parts.
Photo: Derek Shore

Left
There is no mistaking this photo of Buckfastleigh (on the South Devon Railway) for anything other than a preservation era scene, as GWR-liveried small Prairie No.5526 runs light past a pair of BR-blue liveried Class 37 diesel locomotives.

Below left
The North Tyneside Steam Railway, which has its base at the former Tyne & Wear Metro test site, operates along a short running line situated admist stark industrial complexes. This 1993 view shows 1939-built Peckett 0-6-0ST *Ashington No.5* heading two Mk.I suburbans.
Photo: Colour Rail

Bottom left
Arley station now serves as a passing point for services on the Severn Valley Railway. Stanier 8F 2-8-0 No.48773 is seen arriving with a passenger service for Kidderminster (note the express headcode). The LNWR signal box was erected during the preservation era on the site of the original.

Below
Arley station modelled in OO, but with a twist! Peter Smith was commissioned to build this diorama of the preserved station in the guise of Hatley as it appeared in the TV series *Oh Dr Beeching!*
Photo: Kirtley Models

First-hand research

One major advantage with modelling a heritage railway is the ability to make sites visits and explore, study and document everything first-hand. As with modelling a contemporary main line model, a present-day preservation scheme allows you to replicate exactly what you see in front of you, which can be a refreshing change from relying entirely on historical research to recreate a location that no longer exists. What's more, a day trip to a preserved railway, heritage centre or museum makes for an enjoyable experience – all in the name of research!

Modelling an existing preservation site is also aided with the availability of ample online reference; track plans can be derived from aerial views on Google Earth, whilst there are plentiful images available on the internet of these modern day preserved stations, locomotives and rolling stock.

fined to the preservation sites; in their formative years during the 1960s, the stations, infrastructure and rail vehicles of the then-nascent schemes were largely contemporary to the surrounding towns, villages and factories that were situated alongside. However, today's heritage sites are often flanked by new-build housing, modern industrial estates and supermarkets – not to mention examples of 21st century traction and infrastructure where there are main line connections.

Preservation as an era

It is worth noting that the preservation era encompasses a significant proportion of Britain's entire railway history, originating as it did in the 1950s. It is by definition the

Above
Short passenger trains are a hallmark of operations on the main demonstration line at Didcot Railway Centre. Backed by 21st century housing, the WWI-era ROD khaki livery of Churchward Mogul No.5322 contrasts with the GWR and early BR liveries worn by locos and stock stabled around the shed yard.

Centre
The embryonic preservation scheme epitomised in one photo; industrial motive power, grass-strewn track and coaches still in ex-BR blue and grey livery. The early days of the preserved Great Central Railway are recalled in this 1973-dated view.
Photo: Colour Rail

Right
A Gresley A4 hauling a single coach? Such was the *modus operandi* on the former Lochty Private Railway in Fife, where John Cameron operated his A4 No.60009 *Union of South Africa* along a short running line until 1973. The small platform and makeshift engine shed are ripe for modelling.
Photo: Colour Rail

broadest of the eras to which railway modellers can refer; even in is entirety, the British Railways era from Nationalisation in 1948 right through to Privatisation in 1994 accounts for only 46 years. Therefore, although most of the layouts described as being set in the 'preservation era' are present-day depictions, it would be equally valid to model a preservation scene set in the 1970s for instance; perhaps an embryonic enterprise with a small industrial tank engine hauling a single blue and grey BR Mk.I coach along a short grass-strewn running line. Road vehicles and fashion typical of the era could be used to reinforce the time period for the model.

Short passenger train formations
The aforementioned scenario leads us neatly on to another distinct advantage of modelling a heritage railway – that of short train formations. Modellers are often space-starved and therefore the 12+ coaches of main line express formations hauled by Pacific steam locomotives prove

prohibitive. However, heritage railways often employ
large locomotive types on just a handful of coaches; even
the longest railways (such as the North Yorkshire Moors or
Severn Valley) only usually run formations of between six
and eight carriages. Indeed, many smaller operatons have
trains of just two or three coaches (such as the main
demonstration line at Didcot Railway Centre), whilst at
places such as Shildon's Locomotion Museum, passengers
are conveyed up and down the demonstration line in just
a single brake van! Such examples are a tremedous boon
to the space-starved modeller.

Just supposing…

Whilst the focus of this publication is on modelling an
actual heritage railway or operation, there is plenty of
scope for devising a 'just supposing' preservation scheme,
perhaps by choosing a closed station or section of a rail
route that in reality evaded a successful preservation bid.
The model could depict how a heritage operation may
have developed, complete with modern infrastructure.
The locomotives and stock could even include examples
that themselves escaped the hands of preservationists,
which would expand the 'just supposing' theme further.

Or how about choosing a preservation bid that floun-
dered, but modelling the scheme as it could have been had
its fortunes been different – such as supposing Dinting
Railway Centre remained open, or that the South Devon
Railway retained its original running line to the terminus
at Ashburton?

Proprietary models

Modellers working in OO and N are well served when it comes to depicting the preservation scene. The ready-to-run manufacturers such as Hornby, Bachmann and Dapol, have released numerous locomotive models over the years in the guises of preserved examples. These have even included some of the spurious liveries that have been seen during the preservation era, such as the Great Central Railway's ex-BR 9F 2-10-0 No.92214 in BR lined green as *Leicester City/Central Star* by Bachmann in OO (in BR days No.92214 was never named and only carried unlined black livery), and one of the Lakeside & Haverthwaite Railway's pair of BR-built Fairburn 2-6-4Ts in an interpretation of pre-Grouping Caledonian Railway lined blue livery (these locomotives only ever wore BR black) by Graham Farish in N.

The Skaledale and Scenecraft ranges of resin 'ready-to-plant' structures (produced by Hornby and Bachmann respectively) have often included suites of structures (signal boxes, station buildings, footbridges etc) from preserved locations such as; Rothley (Great Central Railway), Highley (Severn Valley Railway), Woody Bay (Lynton & Barnstaple Railway) and Goathland (North Yorkshire Moors Railway).

Next steps

This introduction has provided a brief overview of the key aspects that make modelling the preservation era an appealing proposition. In the following chapters we present some of the best heritage railway layouts built by enthusiasts in recent years, followed by an exploration of many real-life heritage sites that would make ideal layouts in their own right. Each is detailed with a scale plan prepared using Peco Streamline geometry as a guide, and both standard and narrow gauge lines are covered. The final chapter examines some model-making projects which specifically relate to recreating the preservation era.

Whilst this publication seeks to provide a suitable springboard from which you will be able to develop your own project, there are, however, no hard and fast rules and it is ultimately down to your own ingenuity and imagination to succeed in creating a satisfying model.

Above
The long-since defunct Dinting Railway Centre was a hive of activity during the 1970s. How about creating a present-day portrayal, which supposes the preservation scheme didn't flounder? The Bachmann Scenecraft resin engine shed could provide an ideal starting point for such a project in 4mm scale.
Photo: Colour Rail

Above and right
Sheffield Park station on the Bluebell Railway formed the basis for a suite of Bachmann Scenecraft structures in N gauge. The main station building pictured here is supplied as three separate modules.

Below and below right
Examples of Bachmann OO gauge models that have been presented in unauthentic liveries carried by preserved locomotives; BR 9F 2-10-0 No.92214 in BR lined green (named *Leicester City/Central Star*) and Fairburn 2-6-4T No.42085 in lined Caledonian blue livery.
Photos: Courtesy Bachmann Europe Plc

Chapter 1

The birth of the UK's preservation movement

The desire to preserve aspects of our railway heritage and the many relics which are a part of it dates back to the very birth of the railway age itself. Even before the first public railway enterprise, the Stockton to Darlington Railway, opened in 1825, primitive steam locomotives were operating on mine railway networks, the most celebrated being Wylam Colliery in Northumberland.

The colliery was owned by Christopher Blackett and began using engines designed and built by William Hedley and Timothy Hackworth around 1815. The names by which these pioneering engines became known, were of course, *Puffing Billy* and *Wylam Dilly* and perhaps rather surprisingly these unusual beam-engines-on-wheels survive to this day, in the Science Museum and the National Museum of Scotland respectively. *Wylam Dilly* was actually still supposedly earning its keep at Craghill Colliery in Scotland until presented to the museum in 1883, nearly 70 years since it had been built.

As one might expect the two relics are static displays, unlikely ever to turn a wheel again, but it is heartening to know that the pair – the oldest surviving steam locomotives in the world – are preserved for posterity, providing proof, if proof were needed, that the spirit of railway preservation was ignited over 200 years ago.

Of course, for decades it was as static displays in museums that the subsequent generations of railway locomotives and associated artefacts deemed worthy of saving for the nation were to find safe refuge. Some railway companies set aside buildings for the specific purpose of preservation, whilst others salted the best examples of their retired workhorses away in discreet corners of their main railway workshops. Others found homes in national or regional civic museums to rest on pedestals.

Most notable of these establishments were those in York and Swindon, with regional collections also housed in Leicester, Birmingham, Glasgow and Clapham. The National Railway Museum was inaugurated in the former NER/LNER/BR locomotive sheds in York in 1975 and combined many of the artefacts previously housed in these disparate locations under one roof.

Despite this national grouping of many preserved engines at a single site, the fierce independence of some of the former regional museums remained intact, and it is

Right
Locomotion No.1 (built 1825) is a pioneer of railway preservation; Its fate was secured in 1857, with it being subsequently displayed at Darlington Top Bank railway station until 1975. It now resides at the town's Head of Steam museum.
Photo: Steve Flint

Below
Early days on the Severn Valley Railway. With BR steam still extant in the north of the country, preserved Ivatt 2MT No.46443 departs Bridgnorth for Hampton Loade on 14 April 1968.
Photo: Bill Wright

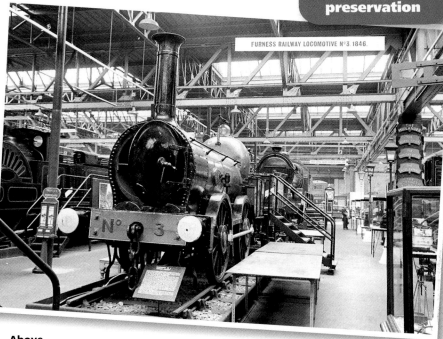

Above
Preserved Furness Railway 0-4-0 No.3 *Coppernob* in the rather cramped surroundings of the erstwhile Museum of British Transport, Clapham in September 1969. Much of the collection was subsequently relocated to York. *Photo: Mike Morant*

Below
A photo taken during the filming of Ealing Studios' *The Titfield Thunderbolt* (released in 1953). The story – inspired by the rebirth of the Talyllyn Railway – follows a group of villagers determined to save and operate their local branch line.
Photo: B King, courtesy Middleton Press

Below right
Barclay 0-4-0WT No.6 *Douglas* is seen at Dolgoch in September 1957 with a Talyllyn Railway Preservation Society Special.
Photo: Colour Rail

still possible to see such iconic engines as Jones' Highland Railway 4-6-0 goods loco in its natural home at Glasgow's Riverside Museum.

Museums apart, the earliest interest in railway preservation really began in the late 1940s when the public, and the railway enthusiasts of the day, began to sit up and question the stealth-like closures of branch lines and associated train service withdrawals that had begun in the 1920s and 1930s.

The decline of rail services, particularly in rural locations, was by then occurring as a result of improvements in road transport, and concern over this state of affairs was steadily infiltrating the public consciousness.

The issue was even examined in the cinema with the release of Ealing Studios' comedy *The Titfield Thunderbolt* in 1953 which portrayed a group of locals banding together to reinstate the local rail service with a motley collection of ageing rolling stock and a Victorian steam engine.

Although a wonderful and entertaining piece of fiction

in its own right, it can equally be considered as a harbinger of the preservation movement that would begin to flourish a decade or so later.

Indeed, concurrent with that movie, a preservation scheme was already well underway in a quiet corner of the British Isles, the vital spark of which had been kindled at the end of WW2 when engineer, author and inland waterways enthusiast Lionel Thomas Caswall Rolt fell upon the remains of the Tallyllyn Railway in Wales.

Spurred on by his earlier memories of past journeys on the Ffestiniog, Welsh Highland and other narrow gauge lines, he journeyed into the small coastal town of Towyn (now Tywyn) in the hope of catching a train up the valley to the railway's terminus at Abergynolwyn.

However on that particular, yet otherwise inauspicious day, he was confronted with a sign on the station gate which read 'No Trains Today'.

Undaunted, his curiosity set him off on foot along the single track line of the railway, up through the cutting out

Above
On 26 April 1958 Double-Fairlie *Taliesin* heads past Boston Lodge on the Festiniog Railway. Built in 1882 and named *Livingston Thompson*, the name *Taliesin* was carried from 1932 – 1961, before the name *Earl of Merioneth* was carried until 1988.
Photo: Colour Rail

of Towyn town station and on past the railway's workshops at Pendre, where he espied a single workman toiling to repair one of the railway's locomotives.

His jaunt continued on through the various small stations and halts along the way until he reached the terminus.

That first visit could easily have slipped from memory had, a little later, Rolt failed to notice in the 1948 Transport Bill – which proposed the nationalisation of Britain's railways – that the diminutive Talyllyn Railway had been omitted from the otherwise very comprehensive inventory of railway companies to be subsumed.

Having witnessed and lamented the disappearance of other such byways, he became so keenly interested in the Talyllyn's future such that he and two other railway-minded friends began a series of visits to Towyn upon which they made the acquaintance of the Talyllyn's owner Sir Henry Haydn Jones and his associate, Edward Thomas.

Despite the dilapidated nature of the railway's assets at that time, it was still running a three day per week summer service and passenger numbers were at record levels. However, the entire future of the line was suddenly thrown into jeopardy with the untimely death of Sir Haydn in July 1950.

Rolt and his two friends, Bill Trinder and Jim Russell, were galvanised into action by Jones' passing and organised a public meeting in Birmingham with the aim of forming a voluntary society to acquire the company outright from Sir Haydn's executors.

The meeting was a tremendous success and the Talyllyn Railway Preservation Society was thus formed. Although it was to be some time before the railway's assets were fully transferred, the first train under the auspices of the new society ran on Whit Monday in 1951.

For Rolt his railway adventure had begun in earnest, but much more significant was that the notion of an enthusiast based railway preservation project had become a reality. The rest, as the old adage goes, is history, and by 1955 the Talyllyn Railway was joined on this very special railway adventure by the Ffestiniog Railway, some 25 miles to the north of Towyn.

A certain Alan Pegler, later to own *Flying Scotsman*, had become that railway's first chairman and trains commenced in the summer of 1955 for the benefit of tourists and enthusiasts.

Meanwhile, and closely mirroring the comic version of events in the movie town of Titfield, enthusiasts and locals had been campaigning to keep open the section of the British Railway route from East Grinstead to Lewes in Sussex.

During the mid 1950s the line had been closed, then reopened under an old statute dating from Railway Acts of the 1870s, only to close again in 1958 after the offending statute was repealed by Parliament. In the

Above
A study in period British fashion at Horsted Keynes on 16 April 1961, with ex-SECR P Class No.27 (left) and venerable – over 70 years of age then – Stroudley Terrier No.55 *Stepney* centre stage. This was the start of the Bluebell's first full year in use.
Photo: Colour Rail

Right
For the first three years of its existence the Bluebell had a link to the outside world via the electrified branch to Haywards Heath via Ardingly, giving rise to sights such as a 2-HAL EMU alongside a P Class in 1962. The branch closed in October 1963.
Photo: Colour Rail

event the Bluebell Railway Preservation Society evolved out of the melee, but its ambitious proposal to reopen the entire route was thwarted, and instead a volunteer operated train service was instigated between Sheffield Park station and Bluebell Halt in 1960. The first passenger carrying standard gauge preserved line in the UK – The Bluebell Railway – had taken to the rails.

Also in 1960, the former Middleton Colliery Railway in the heart of Leeds began service operations under the patronage of volunteers from the Middleton Railway Preservation Society which had been formed by staff and students of Leeds University. Both freight and occasional passenger workings ensued until 1969, from whence passenger trains have continued to operate over the line's 1.5km urban route.

As the decade got underway, the number of preservation proposals and schemes, almost all adopting the

Talyllyn volunteer model, began to grow steadily. The Keighley & Worth Valley Railway scheme was one of the first off the mark, with the formation of its preservation society taking place in 1962, barely six months after closure.

It took a further six years however to acquire suitable stock and obtain its light railway order. The first public train left the curved branch platform en route for the terminus at Oxenhope in June 1968.

Not far behind were; the Severn Valley Railway, inaugurated in 1965 and reopening in 1970; the North Yorkshire Moors Railway, inaugurated in 1967 with the first public trains operating in 1973; the embryonic Great Central Railway, inaugurated under the title of the Main Line Preservation Group in 1968, operated its first train in 1973 at Loughborough; and the North Norfolk Railway which ran its first public train in 1975.

Above
The North Yorkshire Moors Railway was one of serveral heritage lines around the country to purchase obsolete Class 100 DMUs from BR. A two-car set (puchased in 1972) is seen here in 1978 departing Grosmont with a 'National Park Scenic Cruise' wearing an interpretation of LNER green and cream livery. *Photo: Steve Flint*

Top right
There's no doubting the 1977 time frame of this scene, recorded at Grosmont. The pseudo-LNER green livery of the BR-built Peppercorn K1 reflects the appetite during the early years for schemes to disassociate themselves from the national BR network. *Photo: Steve Flint*

Enthusiastic and newly formed societies of volunteers may have been the mainstay of these pioneering heritage lines, but a number of commercial ventures to run tourist railways, and exploit the growing nostalgia of the steam engine, also emerged during this period.

Most notably was the move to preserve that most archetypal of Great Western branch lines; the Ashburton branch, which ran from Totnes on the GW's main line in Devon. The Dart Valley Light Railway Company Ltd was established in 1965 with the aim of operating a profitable tourist railway. Plans however were thwarted by central government which procured the trackbed between Ashburton and Buckfastleigh for land on which to build the then new A38 dual carriageway. Nevertheless the Dart Valley ran its first train in 1969 and hap-

Above
This scene at Loughborough in 1973 is a far cry from the developed Great Central Railway operation we know today, with overgrown track and industrial motive power providing cab rides around the station site. *Photo: Colour Rail*

Left
One that got away; today's South Devon Railway did, for a brief time in the late 1960s stake a claim on the terminus station at Ashburton, until it was cut off following the A38 road modernisation. *Photo: Colour Rail*

Above
In stark contrast the Stanier 8Fs and Black Fives that resided at the former Carnforth MPD (10A) just a few years before, Steamtown Museum was home to several European outline locomotives in the 1970s, including Deutsche Bundesbahn Pacific 012 104-6 (left) and DB 0-6-0T 80.014 (right). Both have since returned to their native Germany as part of the South German Railway collection at Heilbronn.
Photo: Steve Flint

Above right
Steamtown in its heyday, when it was home to main line locomotives including celebrity 4-6-2 No.4472 *Flying Scotsman*, as pictured beneath one of the depot's concrete coaling towers on 11 July 1978.
Photo: Colour Rail

Right
An April 1977 view of Fairburn 2-6-4T No.2085 in elaborate (but entirely unauthentic) lined Caledonian Railway blue livery, seen running round its train at Lake Side on the Lakeside & Haverthwaite Railway. The overall roof was later demolished.
Photo: Steve Flint

pily has been doing so, at least as far as Buckfastleigh and under the management of the South Devon Railway company, ever since.

Other commercial ventures included the establishment of Steamtown at the former Carnforth locomotive depot in 1967. This was actually part of a much grander scheme which intended the operation of the entire reopened branch from Plumpton on the Cumbrian coast route, to Lakeside on the shore of Windermere. These plans were also curtailed by road development, in this case the trunk route to Barrow in Furness – the A590 – leaving only the section from Haverthwaite to the terminus on which to run a service. Operations began in May 1973 and fortunately still operate to this day, though the magnificent overall roof which once adorned the Lakeside terminus is now sadly no more (see page 56).

Following the success of these early schemes through the sixties, the 1970s brought a proliferation of new railway preservation strategies and manifestos. These ranged from purist ventures aimed at recapturing, as authentically as possible, the bygone railway as an object of academic

compliance for enthusiasts, through to commercial ventures with an unashamed agenda for tourist capitalisation.

Examples here in both categories include the opening of the Llangollen Railway in 1975 with barely 20m of running track; the West Somerset Railway – currently the longest heritage railway in the UK – in 1976; the Bala Lake Railway – a narrow gauge line on a former standard gauge route – in 1979; and in 1980, the Brecon Mountain Railway – an unusual combination of overseas narrow gauge stock operating on a former standard gauge trackbed in the Brecon Beacons National Park.

Many of these newer ventures realised, as the earlier established ones were discovering, that in order to pay their way, they had to rely on both of the different financial operational models – voluntary labour and commercial revenue generation.

In other words, in order to satisfy the wishes of those in the intrinsic historical camp, it was also necessary to apply the commercial realities of fund generation. The consequence was that it was not too long before Santa and Thomas the Tank Engine special trains appeared on many of these railways, often with locomotive smokeboxes adorned with physiognomic representations of the fairy tale heroes – much to the chagrin of the doctrinaire enthusiast!

Yet despite this cultural dilemma, tolerance prevailed on both sides, and the railway preservation movement continued to flourish and expand throughout the latter part of the 20th century. Heritage railways in all shapes and sizes emerged; reinstated standard gauge routes, playing host to eclectic collections of motive power, rubbed shoulders with completely new enterprises operating home-grown narrow gauge trains on the trackbeds of long-closed BR routes.

Not all heritage schemes proved to be sustainable. Steamtown at Carnforth (1967) proposed as the aforemen-

tioned Cumbrian centre for steam heritage opertaions, and the Dinting Railway Centre (1968) near Glossop in Derbyshire both closed to the public after several years of activity.

Steamtown has since become the centre for West Coast Railways, the privateer railway leasing firm which provides the carriage stock for many of the heritage specials operating Britain's railway network today. The Dinting operation ceased in 1990 for no other reason than its lease ran out. It had been operated by the Bahamas Locomotive Society, and at one time the site in the locomotive yard adjacent to Dinting Railway station played host to many famous steam engines including the Midland Railway's preserved express 4-4-0 compound No.1000 and Peppercorn's preserved A2 LNER Pacific No.532 *Blue Peter*. Happily, the Bahamas Locomotive Society found a new home at Ingrow on the Keighley & Worth Valley Railway.

Also in the 1960s attempts were made to establish a Somerset & Dorset railway centre in the former S&DJR station at Radstock North station. The preservation of one of the S&DJR 7F 2-8-0 freight engines, then in Woodham's scrapyard, was behind the move and the group spearheading the proposal – The Somerset and Dorset Circle – leased the closed station building and up platform. The locomotive was towed to Radstock in 1970 and later, along with some industrial tank engines in working order, open days took place which included brake van rides a mile along the line to Writhlington Colliery. Plans to buy the station and the line were put forward early in 1974, but fund raising came to nothing. Operations ceased at the site shortly afterwards and the collection of artefacts was split between other groups at other locations. The main group's new base was later established in the old goods yard at Washford, on the West Somerset Railway and still functions to this day (see page 74)

Today many of these heritage centres and lines present a very professional and polished appearance to the visitor, but it wasn't always like that. As we have examined above,

Top
Adorned with festive tinsel and ribbons, No.1450 heads a Santa Special past Hayles Abbey on the Gloucestershire Warwickshire Railway in December 1997.
Photo: Rail Photoprints

Above
Not for the purists! Fowler 3F 0-6-0T No.47327 masquerades as a well-known children's story character during a special event on the Severn Valley Railway in 2012.
Photo: Colour Rail

Below
On 24 September 1978 No.6000 *King George V* and No.6201 *Princess Elizabeth* 'top and tail' a three coach shuttle at the now defunct Bulmers site near Hereford.
Photo: Andrew Burnham

Left
The preservation movement owes much to Woodham's scrapyard at Barry docks for the fleets of ex-BR steam locomotives that have been restored from rusting hulks to fulfill the motive power needs of Britain's heritage railways. This ex-GWR 'Hall' 4-6-0 typifies the condition of most of the locomotives that left the yard.
Photo: Philip Lovell

activities at these sites in the early days were often very *ad hoc*; particularly so in the time before the preservation groups were granted light railway orders, when only society members or invited guests could travel on the trains. Brake vans and open wagons would often be cobbled into a rake of vehicles in which folk travelled at their own risk behind an industrial saddle tank.

Even after the granting of the light railway order, allowing the heritage lines to charge fares, trains would often consist of all sorts of assorted vehicles, safe for travel yes, but sometimes from different historical periods, and in a mix of liveries and varying states of refurbishment. Likewise, the sites themselves would be equally disordered, with sidings full of relics awaiting restoration, some under the cover of tarpaulins, some open to the elements with wood rotting and steel rusting, and all set amidst a carpet of long grass, weeds and shrubs as mother nature attempted to reclaim the area. Even today such vestiges of

Left
A siding full of unrestored locomotives in Bridgnorth yard during the 1970s, at least four of which were purchased from Woodham's.
*Photo: Douglas Tiley
(Craig Tiley collection)*

Below
An early 1970s open day at the former S&DJR Radstock North station, with Hawthorn Leslie 0-6-0ST *Isabel* (Works No.3437) providing brake van rides.
*Photo: Douglas Tiley
(Craig Tiley collection)*

long withdrawn vehicles litter odd corners of the scene, or rest alongside the main running lines blocking the view from the passing carriage windows.

This eclectic and dilapidated appearance of preservation sites, especially so in their early years, has an appeal all of its own. Whilst some railway modellers may prefer to depict a neat and orderly railway, others are inspired to model the rustic charm and chaos which frequently prevails at these localities.

Either way, Britain's heritage railways and visitor sites now number into hundreds and each and every one takes trippers on an enchanting and informative journey through our railway past. Modelling them has also become a significant genre within the vast sphere of the hobby with many layout builders choosing it as a serious theme, some of which are featured amongst the pages which follow.

It's thanks to the efforts and vision of people such as LTC Rolt and those who followed in his footsteps that we now have possibly the most prodigious railway preservation movement in the world.

One wonders also if the writers and producers of *The Titfield Thunderbolt* ever knew what their little parody of railway preservation might unleash. Or perhaps they did?

Above
Robert Stephenson & Hawthorn 0-6-0ST (Works No.7289/WD 71480) heads a motley collection of stock on the K&WVR in 1970.
Photo: Colour Rail

Below
Full circle with Ivatt 2MT No.41241, which received its former K&WVR red livery in 2018 to mark the line's 50th year of preservation.
Photo: Joseph Connell

Chapter 2

Standard gauge heritage railways

Of the hundreds of standard gauge preservation schemes that exist across Great Britain, the majority – by a significant margin – can be categorised as heritage railways, where the main focus is concerned with the reviving of train services along former rail routes. This is in contrast to railway centres and museums (the subject of Chapter 3), where running trains is often secondary to the preservation of locomotives, rolling stock and other artefacts of historical significance.

Below
There are a few heritage lines that occupy former main line routes. The preserved Great Central Railway is unique, however, with its double track.

Right
Standard gauge heritage railways in model form: an eclectic mix of stock on show at Northbridge station on Warley MRC's fictitious Dalton Valley Railway.

During the early pioneering days of railway preservation, there was often so much impetus placed on getting a viable train operation up and running that many schemes utilised whatever stock was available to them, regardless of its authenticity for the route being revived. There are countless examples of former British Railways lines being graced by examples of industrial motive power, or former BR locomotives operating far away from their natural habitats (such as ex-GWR Dukedog No.9017 on the Bluebell Railway in Sussex, or Maunsell S15s operating through the North Yorkshire Moors).

Often the use of industrial motive power presented an economical option – especially when running lines were short and train formations consisted of a couple of carriages. Furthermore, many industrial locomotives were available directly from private companies in working order, enabling them to be put straight to use on heritage line duties, without the need for the expensive overhauls or restoration work that was often required for former main-line locomotives.

As many heritage schemes developed, with running lines extended and longer trains, many of these industrial stalwarts became insufficient for coping with the expanded operational needs and were displaced by larger ex-BR locomotives. Such was the situation on lines including the West Somerset, Severn Valley and East Lancs. However, many of the smaller heritage lines that exist today can still rely on small industrial locomotive types to form the back-

Above
Ex-BR(W) Dukedog No.9017 pictured in 1963 at the Bluebell Railway in Sussex, a long way from its native North Wales stomping ground.
Photo: Mike Morant

Top right
A pair of ex-Lambton Colliery 0-6-2Ts were a staple of NYMR services in the railway's early years.
Photo: Steve Flint

Right
After its reliance on industrials in its formative years, the West Somerset Railway went on to establish a pool of ex-BR locomotives.

Below
The Avon Valley Railway continues to make good use of industrial locomotive types to satisfy its motive power needs.

Left
Some heritage lines have looked further afield for suitable motive power. This Polish-built 0-6-0T is owned by the Swindon & Cricklade Railway, presenting a very different scene to the locomotive types that would have operated along this former Midland & South Western Junction Railway route prior to preservation.
Photo: Steve King

bone of their motive power needs, which underlines the immense contribution that former industrial locomotives have made (and continue to make) to the preservation movement.

It isn't just with the locomotives and rolling stock that heritage railways have often been found to disregard historical authenticity in favour of operational necessity; many former station sites have been restored to conditions far from their original layouts and facilities. Take Cranmore on the East Somerset Railway or Sheffield Park on the Bluebell Railway for instance; both are former branch line stations that have become established locomotive and engineering headquarters for their respective railways, which consequently means the sites have been developed by preservationists to include the additional infrastructure this use requires, including running sheds and maintenance workshops.

Above
The Foxfield Railway occupies a former industrial railway system, which means locomotives such as this Bagnall 0-6-0ST (No.2221 *Lewisham*) are more appropriate to the heritage operations than ex-BR classes.
Photo: Phil Barnes

Left
David Shepherd, the late founder of the East Somerset Railway, oversaw the construction of this two-road brick running shed at Cranmore, to house his two ex-BR tender locomotives. The platform in the foregound was also constructed in preservation era.
Photo: Phil Barnes

Above

Sheffield Park station is the operational base of the Bluebell Railway. The site has been much transformed from its original pre-preservation configuration; the south end of the site (as seen here from the station footbridge) is occupied by extensive locomotive workshop and display facilities.

There are exceptions however, such as Carrog on the Llangollen Railway, which was the subject of a painstaking restoration to near-original c.1950s condition. Despite this former rural branch station serving for many years as the western terminus of this heritage line, efforts were made to ensure the infrastructure did not evolve beyond what was there originally; this is easier said than done when the station is expected to cater for the sudden influxes of hundreds of passengers that alight from heritage services whilst providing the amenities that are commensurate with today's tourism industry.

And what of the stations that never even existed origi-

Right

Carrog station on the Llangollen Railway is a superb example of an authentic station restoration. This scene, which encapsulates much that the UK's preservation movement strives to achieve, is replete with appropriate motive power; Dukedog No.9017 (which operated along the Barmouth – Ruabon route in BR days) returned to the North Wales line in 2009 for a gala event.

nally – such as Harman's Cross on the Swanage Railway or Kidderminster on the Severn Valley; both are complete preservation-era fabrications built to satisfy the unique operational needs of the respective heritage operations, with no links to the history of the respective routes that they serve. However, it is testament to the work of those involved with their construction, that both of these examples exhibit extraordinary attention to authentic styling, which belies their recent construction.

All of the anachronisms and unlikely juxtapositions that can be discovered across the heritage railway movement provide huge modelling potential. How about recreating the early years of the preserved Great Central Railway with former GNR Stirling Single No.1 hauling a handful of BR

Top
It is hard to believe that the Severn Valley Railway's Kidderminster terminus didn't exist prior to preservation. Built on a former goods yard site, the new station opened in 1984.

Above right
Harmans Cross is a convincing recreation of a Southern passing station, opened in 1989 on the Swanage Railway.
Photo: Graham Hutton

Right
An unlikely combination of loco, stock and location sees GNR Stirling Single No.1 head a rake of BR Mk.I coaches on the Great Central Railway in 1982.
Photo: Mike Morant

Mk.I coaches? Or how about the Nene Valley Railway with its mix of British and overseas locomotives and coaching stock? Whilst purists may decry such conflicts of historical authenticity, from a modelling perspective there is plenty to inspire.

In this chapter we present a selection of layouts based on both real heritage railways and fictitious creations, from a faithful interpretation of Horsted Keynes on the Bluebell Railway, to a convincing rendition of the supposed Dalton Valley Railway. These are accompanied by a series of prototype plans that cover a range of different layout formats, from a terminus to fiddle yard scheme based on the Swanage Railway, to a U-shaped room filler that includes both of the termini on the Lakeside & Haverthwaite Railway.

This is, however, only a small snapshot of the potential layout schemes that can be derived using the standard gauge heritage lines of Great Britain as a basis, so why not visit your nearest preserved railway and see what modelling potential it has to offer?

Left
Demonstration freights are a feature of special events at many heritage railways. Fowler 7F 2-8-0 No.88 (in pseudo-S&DJR lined Prussian blue livery) departs Toddington on the GWSR with a mixed rake of wagons.

Above
Many heritage railways that traditionally utilise steam locomotives, do occasionally stage diesel gala events. Here visiting Deltic D9009 *Alycidon* looks rather out of place as it ambles along the Bluebell Railway (a far cry its former East Coast Main Line haunts), with an assorted rake of coaches, including Bulleid designs.
Photo: Phil Barnes

Below
The Nene Valley Railway has cultivated a reputation for running European locos and stock in harmony with British prototypes; here a Class 56 heads a rake of Danish coaching stock.
Photo: Rail Photoprints

Goathland
The North Yorkshire Moors Railway

Left
The Lambton 0-6-2T (constructed using an R-T-R LNER J72 mechanism) has charge of the railway's restored NER snow plough.

Below
The distinctive stepped-gable station buildings were available as Skaledale resin structures from Hornby, saving hours of build time.

Above
Faithful replicas of the NYMR fleet, such as No.926 *Repton* (complete with extended tender raves) appear in miniature on the layout.

Constructed in OO by Simon & Hannah Denham

*Goathland will be recognisable to many as 'Aidensfield' from the
TV show* Heartbeat, *and 'Hogsmeade' in the Harry Potter films. In
reality it is a passing station on the preserved North Yorkshire
Moors Railway, which runs for 18 miles from Pickering to Grosmont
(where high-season through trains also operate via a main line
connection to Whitby).*

*Originally opened in 1836 as the Whitby & Pickering Railway, the
route closed in 1965 as part of the Beeching cuts, but was reopened
in 1973 by the North York Moors Historical Railway Trust Ltd.*

*Much of the original infrastructure survives in near original
condition, including the main station buildings, coal drops and
goods shed (now a tea room). The site has been restored as close
as possible to c.1922 North Eastern Railway condition. The NER
pattern footbridge has, however, been erected since preservation.*

The layout described

*Occupying an area measuring 12' x 8', the layout has been
configured as a continuous run with a single fiddle yard along the
back. (This was in preference to having a fiddle yard at each end,
which would have necessitated a prohibitive overall length for the
space available.) Configuring the layout as a continuous run also
simplifies the operation, negating any need to turn or reverse
trains in the fiddle yard.*

*Compression of the station site has been undertaken to fit the
available space, including a reduction in the platform lengths.
Accordingly, shorter train lengths are used of five carriages, instead
of the seven or eight on the real NYMR.*

*The majority of the station buildings are from the Hornby
Skaledale range and all trackwork is Peco Streamline code 100,
whilst locomotives and rolling stock are largely from the Bachmann
Branchline and Hornby ranges.*

*Great effort has been taken to represent the actual locomotives
and coaches that can be seen on the real NYMR, including models
of Lambton Tank No.29 and WD 2-10-0 No.3672* Dame Vera Lynn *–
neither of which are currently available ready-to-run; the latter was
adapted from a Bachmann WD 2-8-0. However, the railway's BR
green-liveried Riddles 2-6-4T No.80135 (an unauthentic
preservation-era livery) is a standard Bachmann product. Similarly,
models of Gresley A4 Pacific No.60007* Sir Nigel Gresley *in BR lined
blue with early emblems, and BR Standard 4MT 2-6-0 No.76079 in
BR lined black with early emblems, were available 'off the shelf'
from Hornby and Bachmann respectively.*

*The layout is digitally controlled using a laptop and Hornby
Railmaster software, which connects to the layout using a Hornby
eLink. Simon & Hannah use iPads as wireless handheld controllers.
Point and signal operation is also digitally controlled on the laptop
with a mimic diagram drawn using the Railmaster software.*

*The layout is full of cameos that reinforce the preservation era
theme, including; an ice cream van and barrel music organ in the
station car park, together with lineside photographers and a model
of the new station shop. Also faithfully represented on the model
are the camping coaches parked behind platform 2.*

Above
Five coach trains can be accommodated
in the loop, compared to seven or eight
on the real thing. A pair of Black Fives
depart with a Pickering-bound train.

Below
The typical NER design of footbridge
was also available in the Hornby
Skaledale range. *Layout photos by
Derek Shore except where stated.*

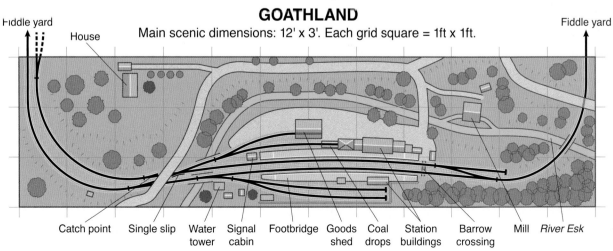

GOATHLAND
Main scenic dimensions: 12' x 3'. Each grid square = 1ft x 1ft.

Fiddle yard

House

Fiddle yard

Catch point   Single slip   Water tower   Signal cabin   Footbridge   Goods shed   Coal drops   Station buildings   Barrow crossing   Mill   *River Esk*

Left
A Class 26-hauled demonstration freight train climbs the gradient to the station. Note the brake van behind the engine: freight workings on heritage railways often run with a van at each end to simplify the run-round procedure at each end of the line.

Right
WD 2-10-0 *Dame Vera Lynn* (modified from a Bachmann WD 2-8-0 model) is stabled a safe distance from camera crews and extras (including a couple of mods) during filming for a *Heartbeat* episode.

Below
A4 Pacific *Sir Nigel Gresley* crosses a BR Standard Class 4 4-6-0 in the station. Heritage railways without turntables or turning triangles involve a lot of tender-first running.
Photo: Steve Flint

Bottom right
Crowds are gathered around the snack van rather than the BR 2-6-4T. No.80136 has been a regular performer on the preserved NYMR.

Horsted Keynes

The Bluebell Railway

Above
Class E4 0-6-2T No.473 *Birch Grove*, models of which have been produced ready-to-run from Bachmann. *Layout photos: Matt Wickham*

Right
The SECR H Class 0-4-4T could be represented in ready-to-run form by the Hornby replica, and the LSWR Adams Radial by either the Hornby or Oxford Rail version.

Constructed in OO by Matt Wickham

The Bluebell Railway in Sussex was founded in 1960, becoming the world's first preserved standard gauge passenger line. Running on part of the former London, Brighton & South Coast Railway route between Lewes and East Grinstead, the Bluebell currently runs for 11 miles between Sheffield Park and East Grinstead (where there is a main line connection with the national network).

Built in 1882, Horsted Keynes was originally a junction station with a branch to Haywards Heath via Ardingly, which accounts for the five platforms and extensive goods facilities that the station once boasted.

Horsted Keynes now serves as a busy intermediate passing point for Bluebell Railway services, with much of the original architecture still in situ and beautifully preserved – including the distinctive passenger subways that connect the platforms. It is also home to the railway's extensive carriage restoration facilities, with the surviving branch spur and adjacent sidings used for storing items of rolling stock awaiting restoration.

Matt was inspired to build a model of Horsted Keynes following family trips to the Bluebell Railway. Buildings are a mixture of resin Skaledale, modified card and plastic kits, as well as some scratchbuilt examples. Station details such as the water cranes were constructed

from 5&9 Models whitemetal kits – a specialist supplier of LB&SCR items.

The track is all Peco Streamline code 100 with medium radius turnouts, powered by SEEP point motors, with the layout controlled by a Morley twin track controller.

Locomotives are a mix of kitbuilt, modified R-T-R, or straight out of the box from the various manufacturers. Rolling stock is mainly R-T-R, with some built from kits, although Matt has also completed a number of 3D-printed vehicles that he designed himself.

Notes on the plan

The scenic section of the layout measures 11' x 7' – the platform lengths having been compressed (they can take four coaches plus a locomotive) to bring the station site down to a practical overall length in 4mm scale. The layout is housed in a garden shed and takes the form of a continuous run, with the running lines from each end of the scenic section curving round to connect to a fiddle yard on the opposite side. (The curved sections are in fact located outside the main structure of the shed, with the running lines exiting through cut-outs in the end walls.)

HORSTED KEYNES

Scenic dimensions: 11' 7" x 2' 2". Each grid square = 1ft x 1ft.

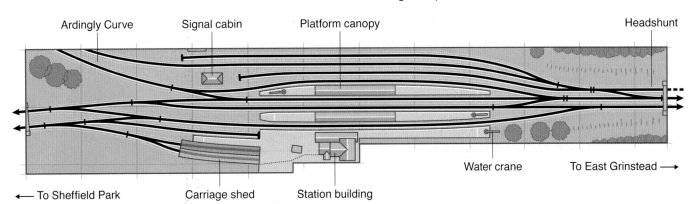

Ardingly Curve   Signal cabin   Platform canopy   Headshunt

Water crane   To East Grinstead →

← To Sheffield Park   Carriage shed   Station building

Above

The spacious site in reality, with its distinctive double-faced down platform (No.5) and the two islands beyond. Access is via ramped subways.

Above right

The signal box used Saxby & Farmer equipment, but was designed by the LBSC itself, along with the buildings on the route.

Right

This view of *Birch Grove* shows it in the same platform on the layout as the Bulleid coach in the photo of the rail station, but further along it.

Below

The H Class again, with Bulleid stock. The ability of modern R-T-R manufacturers to reproduce pre-Group liveries makes a layout such as this more achievable.

Above

Rolling stock is an eclectic mix, produced using many items from ready-to-run models to home-made self-designed 3D prints.

Left

The Bluebell is home to a number of unique survivors, thanks to its early establishment; locos such as the Dukedog were able to be saved. The model is available ready-to-run from Bachmann.

Above right

The former *Birch Grove* now seen in early Southern Railway garb with the tiny B prefix to its number, denoting Brighton. It is about to depart south for the railway's terminus at Sheffield Park.

Right

The line's two antique Terriers – *Fenchurch* in the lined Marsh umber and *Stepney* in original and elaborate Stroudley ochre livery, coupled bunker-to-bunker in the bay at Horsted Keynes.

Left

The author's model of *Fenchurch*, leaving the station with an observation saloon.

Northbridge

Based on the Severn Valley Railway

Below
The Western and rake of Great Western Collett coaches channels the Severn Valley aura very well.
All photos: Steve Flint

Below
Steam and diesel locomotives are housed in a
purpose-built modern shed. The layout allows models of
locomotives that were not preserved – or exist as static
exhibits – to be seen in action.

Northbridge (Dalton Valley Railway) Overall size of scenic section 9700mm x 800mm. Each grid square = 300mm x 300mm.

Constructed by members of Warley Model Railway Club in OO

We wanted to create what would be for each of us, our first
exhibition layout. We all owned quantities of 4mm OO gauge rolling
stock, but that was about as far as it went, for we each came to the
group with a very wide range of diverse model railway interests.
So the first question was how would we build a layout that could
cover everything from pre-Grouping Highland Railway, Big Four GWR,
British Railways steam, and diesel types from the 1970s to the 2010s?
The answer is of course: build a heritage railway layout. The Severn
Valley Railway is fairly local to us in the West Midlands and seemed
like a suitable prototype, but it was problematical for two main
reasons. Firstly, we are all aware of the rivet-counters out there in the
wider domain of the hobby and there is nothing less certain than they
would gather like moths to a flame if we attempted to do an exact
copy of one of the SVR stations.

Secondly, as it was to be an exhibition layout, it had to have
entertainment value for the viewers and we reckoned that a layout
faithful to the SVR would not provide enough interest. So we
compromised and decided to use the station at Bridgnorth as the
basis, but with several twists to catch the eye and to be more visually
entertaining.

Thus, Northbridge was born, and when the kindly aforementioned
rivet counters point out that Bridgnorth is "...not like that!" we can
agree and point out politely that it is in fact Northbridge. In the
event, apart from the station building, very little else resembles the
Bridgnorth site.

We upgraded the line to double track and added a branch line, all
to give more options for train movements. The turntable has been
added and sits to the left of the engine shed. We also added a
turntable and a goods yard to allow some shunting, both by group
members and by the public at shows.

Hopefully with all these options there will always be something
moving. Of course there are those out there who appreciate finescale
models of sleepy little branch lines operating to authentic timetables
which might see one train movement an hour, but our aim is to keep
the paying public entertained with lots of train movements.
Consequently, consideration for viewer expectations was a key
criterion when planning the layout.

The main station building and the engine shed were both
scratchbuilt and based on originals at Bridgnorth. We struck lucky
with both, as the SVR had applied for planning permission to alter the
two of them and scale plans were readily accessible at the local
council planning office.

We do try to keep operation within reasonable bounds, but trains
that were never preserved, such as the Blue Pullman are allowed to
visit Northbridge. We can certainly call on a stock list that would
make any manager of a present-day British heritage railway green
with envy, particularly as ours don't require major fund raising efforts
and regular boiler rebuilds! The stock comprises many R-T-R items, as
well as kitbuilt ones and some scratchbuilt examples.

(Abridged from the article by Duncan Petford, RM December 2018.)

Above
The five-road shed provides covered accommodation: a far cry from the early days of preservation, when much was stored out in the open.

Right
Rebuilt Bulleid Pacific *Sir Keith Park* is about to be coaled using the typical method of using a grab bucket on a jib; old-school coaling plants are few and far between.

Below
Active in the 1960s as part of a rare collection of Scottish locomotives, the real Highland Railway Jones Goods is now a museum piece. But not in model form!

Left
The station buildings were scratchbuilt by Jim Smith from originals obtained via the local council planning department (and see also RM June 2018).

Above
Trains await departure as others are prepared. As with the Severn Valley, the Dalton Valley Railway has several rakes of pre-nationalisation stock.

Below
The BR Standard Class 4 2-6-4Ts have proved their worth on many real railways, and more of the type await restoration from scrapyard state.

Sheaf station

The Sheaf Valley Railway

Constructed in N by Oliver Reading

With a scenic section measuring just 8' x 1', the Sheaf Valley Railway is a compact portrayal of a fictional preserved railway terminus. A preservation theme was adopted to utilise Oliver's mixed collection of N gauge locomotive and rolling stock models to best advantage, which covers a wide variety of steam and diesel prototypes. Locomotives are from the Graham Farish and Dapol ranges and Oliver was keen to ensure that they are models of locomotives actually living 'in captivity', or represent classes that have a preserved example (and are gradually being renumbered accordingly). Some of the locomotives have been fitted with sound.

The station buildings are from the Market Hampton series of resin structures formerly available in the Bachmann Scenecraft range, whilst the water tower is a Hornby Lyddle End item. The platform, which can accommodate three coaches, was constructed from Metcalfe card kits.

The layout plays on many of the visual contrasts seen at preservation sites around the UK; original structures (including the station building and water tower) stand alongside modern buildings (such as the extensive locomotive workshops), whilst BR blue-liveried diesels can be seen on adjacent lines to steam locomotives in pre-Nationalisation colours.

Oliver has fully exploited the potential offered with modelling a preservation theme; adopting a supposed former South Yorkshire branch terminus as a basis, but with large mainline locomotive types hauling short trains – such as new-build Peppercorn A1 No.60163 Tornado heading a demonstration mail train composed of just three vehicles.

Notable details include the station's catering facilities, which takes the form of an LNER Gresley Buffet Car permanently parked at the end of a siding, and rows of stored rolling stock items in various states of disrepair awaiting restoration. Such cameos help to reinforce the preservation theme.

The layout is configured for digital control using the Bachmann Dynamis system and Peco Code 55 track has been used throughout. Automatic uncoupling is achieved with Dapol 'Easi-Shunt' couplings, activated by permanent magnets set within the track at strategic locations around the layout. The fiddle yard adds a further 4' to the overall length of the layout, bringing the total length to 12'.

Above
As with real preserved railways, early morning and late evening services are in the hands of DMUs.
All photos: Derek Shore

Below
The shadows cast by characters created by the Revd. Awdry is a large one: the Thompson B1 4-6-0 is on 'Thomas' duty today.

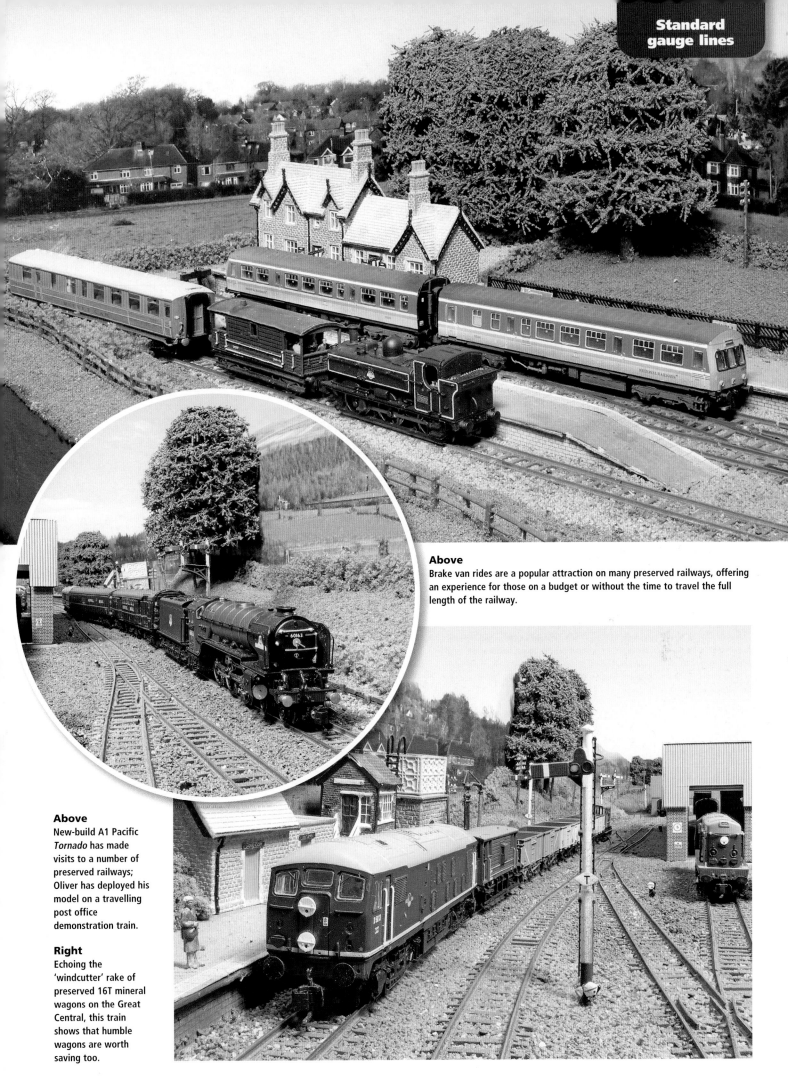

Above
Brake van rides are a popular attraction on many preserved railways, offering an experience for those on a budget or without the time to travel the full length of the railway.

Above
New-build A1 Pacific *Tornado* has made visits to a number of preserved railways; Oliver has deployed his model on a travelling post office demonstration train.

Right
Echoing the 'windcutter' rake of preserved 16T mineral wagons on the Great Central, this train shows that humble wagons are worth saving too.

Above
Tornado arrives at the terminus of the Sheaf Valley Railway with another trainload of passengers. The station buildings were obtained from the Bachmann Scenecraft range.

Below
Their time will come… an 0-6-0PT and tender await restoration, whilst a couple of newly-arrived ex-main line coach B4 bogies are checked over prior to re-use.

Right
Many preserved lines have links to the national network, allowing railtours to visit, thereby enhancing revenue. A GWR Hall departs the terminus for the main line.

Above
A Class 37 and Class 26 prepare to take on fuel as an Ivatt Class 2 Mogul departs the terminus tender-first. Semaphore signals are the Dapol working models.

SHEAF VALLEY

Station building   Toilets   Signal box   Water tower   Overall size: 12' x 1'. Each grid square = 1 sq ft.   Fiddle yard

Loco depot   Carriage shed

Carrog

The Llangollen Railway

Constructed in N by Gordon Crapper

Carrog station has been beautifully restored to c.1950s BR (Western Region) condition and now serves as a passing point for passenger services on the Llangollen Railway, which operates along a 10 mile section of the former GWR route between Barmouth and Ruabon.

Gordon chose Carrog as the subject of a model because the heritage railway is situated close to where he lives, which made first-hand research very easy. N gauge was chosen for reasons of space; it is stored in a cupboard and sits on a dining table when in use, which means it also had to be lightweight. The baseboard was formed of a 4' x 2' piece of 6mm MDF, braced with 34mm x 18mm battens.

The positions of the buildings and other key structures were first sketched out on the baseboard, with track then laid using Peco Setrack for the first radius curves, and Streamline flexible track through the station and in the fiddle yard loop. Second radius points were used in the station and the loop, first radius elsewhere.

The photographic backscene was created using a panorama taken from the station footbridge. The layout features two tunnel mouths to serve as exits from the scenic section; these don't feature in real life but photos of Berwyn tunnel (further east along the Llangollen Railway) were used to create the portals. The hillsides were built up from cereal packets, covered with grass mat, powder scatters and lots of trees and bushes.

Locomotives and rolling stock

Gordon chooses to run the layout in its present-day revival, but with a few minor changes it could represent any period in the station's history. Gordon has been able to use many proprietary models to depict the railway's locomotives and rolling stock including an Ixion Manor 4-6-0, together with a Graham Farish BR Standard 2-6-4T, GWR large Prairie and Fowler 3F 0-6-0T. Aside from rakes of Graham Farish BR Mk.Is, he also has a selection of wagons for demonstration goods trains and to park in the sidings as on the real thing, along with an old coach.

Operation

Gordon can either just let the trains run round the circuit, or he can follow a printed running order which uses all the stock a couple of times as a sort of 'steam gala'. In this case it is supposed that the fiddle yard loop becomes 'Corwen', and down trains run round there. Up trains run into the long headshunt, which is in effect Llangollen station. The train can then depart again with another locomotive or be backed into a siding and another train pulled out. There will always be a train in one Carrog platform, waiting to cross the next in the other direction.
Layout photography by Gordon Crapper

Below
An overall view of the compact layout, showing how the Carrog station site has been reconfigured into a circular format.

Below
Carrog station has been painstakingly restored to near original c.1950s BR Western Region condition. The former goods yard is used by the heritage railway to store permanent way and track maintenance vehicles.

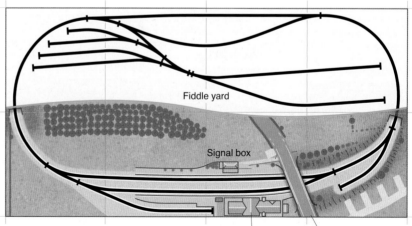

CARROG
Overall size: 4' x 2'. Each grid square 1ft x 1ft.

Fiddle yard

Signal box

Station house   Road bridge

Making the buildings using photographs

Gordon describes how he made the structures for his layout:

"I had plenty of photographs of the station buildings and decided that, if I took more of them from good front-on positions, I could arrange them into flat elevations which I could print off on my desktop printer. The elevations could then be cut out and glued together exactly as one would with a commercially-produced card kit. The station house is now someone's home, so I was careful not to trespass, and parts of the back of the house are guesswork from bits showing on the photographs I could take.

The model buildings would need to be selectively compressed in order to fit the available space on the board.

The road bridge dominates the station, and its size was calculated using standard dimensions on the N Gauge Society's website. I made some plain paper cut-outs first and checked that N gauge rolling stock would pass through.

The dimensions of buildings were then estimated by comparing the relative heights of doors in relationship to the height of the bridge. I also did this for the signal box. Counting and comparing the brick courses in the photos helped to bring everything to a common scale. The sizes of all the component images were resized on my computer screen using photo manipulation software*.

Taking the road overbridge as an example, my original photograph (photo A) needed a fair amount of work to arrive at a suitable form. This included removing the signal, various trees, and replacing parts below platform level with pieces imported from other photographs taken from much closer. Using the crop, cloning and resizing tools I eventually had a final image of the complete bridge elevation to scale. Likewise the opposite elevation was prepared in the same way and assembled into a sheet ready for printing (photo B). Once printed onto thin card, the parts were cut out and curved to shape. Thin ply sub-walls were cut out to provide rigidity as shown (photo C) and the printed sides attached with glue (photo D).

A lot of similar computer work was required to make a line-up of front, side and back elevations of the buildings. During the process I made some interim prints to check dimensions and fit etc (photo D). Once I was satisfied, the full images were prepared and printed (photo E) all ready for cutting out and assembly.

Some of the smaller buildings have a plywood sub-structure, to provide rigidity, but for the station house and tea room, such a sub-structure would be too complex, so I used cereal packet card as a cardboard inner layer for rigidity. The main print-out was glued to this and when dry the laminate was cut out, folded and assembled. Some extra gable ends, to make cross-members to strengthen the structure, and bay windows were printed as well (photo F). I also printed all the small notices; some are tiny, but still legible. "

*Although Adobe Photoshop is widely used for this, other photo manipulation software is just as usable, such as GIMP, Sumopaint, Paint.net etc, all of which are downloadable from the internet.

Bodmin General

PROTOTYPE FEATURE
The Bodmin & Wenford Railway

Below
The station buildings appear largely in original condition. The carmine and cream BR Mk.I provides refreshment facilities.
Photo: Mark Lynam

The prototype described

Situated in Cornwall, Bodmin General was constructed by the Great Western Railway as a branch junction terminus; one line connecting with the GW main line at Bodmin Road (a distance of 3½ miles) and another line to Boscarne Junction (a distance of 3 miles). The latter was opened in 1888 and connected with the existing LSWR-owned Bodmin & Wadebridge Railway.

Passenger services ceased during the late 1960s, with freight traffic continuing between Bodmin Road and Wadebridge until 1978.

Following subsequent closure of the route, the line from Bodmin Road (now Parkway) to Boscarne Junction, via Bodmin General, was purchased for preservation. The first open day was held in 1986, with passenger trains commencing between Bodmin General and Bodmin Parkway from 1990, and the line to Boscarne Junction from 1996.

Bodmin General station exists with much of the infrastructure and track layout existing as per its original BR(W) condition. However, the locomotive shed was demolished c.1974, with a modern structure built in its place. A stock shed was also constructed on the site formerly occupied by the goods shed, this structure also having been demolished.

Passenger services have been handled by a variety of locomotive types during the preservation era, both steam and diesel. Notable examples of steam traction include; Beattie 2-4-0WTs Nos.30585 and 30587, ex-GWR small Prairie 2-6-2T No.5552, ex-GWR 2-8-0T No.4247, ex-GWR 0-6-0PT No.4612 and the pair of Port of Par Bagnall 0-4-0STs – Alfred and Judy. Moving to the other end of the spectrum, new-build A1 Pacific No.60163 Tornado has also visited the railway. Nearly all of these locomotives are available as ready-to-run items in 4mm scale.

Notes on the plan

The station layout has been drawn to scale, which works out at 13'6" for the scenic section. Some selective compression could be undertaken to reduce this by 18" to 2', without any detrimental effect on train lengths or operational scope. Beacon Road bridge forms a natural scenic break at the station throat end of the plan, providing a foil to the two branches as they run off the scenic section. In reality the two lines diverge away from each other but it would be practical to keep them parallel after the bridge to enable them to run into a shared fiddle yard.

Below
Photographed from Beacon Road bridge, a former BR Type 3 leaves the station with a rake of carmine and cream Mk.Is. Note the BR Mk.III parked on the left outside the back of the running shed, which is used to provide volunteer accommodation. *Photo: Mark Lynam*

Right
The railway has established restoration workshops at Bodmin General, with this modern corrugated structure occupying part of the former station yard. Locomotives under restoration and general 'clutter' make for tantalising subjects of modelling projects.
Photo: Mark Lynam

Below
Seen from the station platform, Small Prairie No.5552 is shunting a rake of coaches with Beacon Road bridge visible in the background. The branch to Boscarne Junction diverges to the right of the train, just by the rear coach.
Photo: Phil Barnes

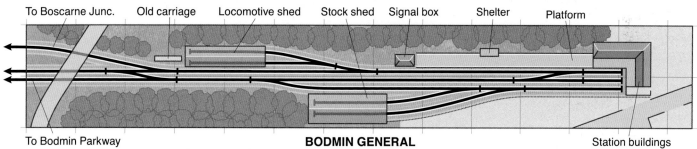

To Boscarne Junc.   Old carriage   Locomotive shed   Stock shed   Signal box   Shelter   Platform

To Bodmin Parkway   **BODMIN GENERAL**   Station buildings
Scenic length: 13' 6". Each grid square 1ft x 1ft.

Ropley
PROTOTYPE FEATURE
The Mid-Hants Railway

Below
With the wheel drop shed just visible to the left, Maunsell U Class No.31806 departs with an up train for Alton, whilst BR Standard Class 5 No.73096 stands alongside prior to returning to the shed yard.

The prototype described

Ropley station was originally an intermediate station on the Mid-Hants line, a secondary route operated by the London & South Western Railway to connect Alton and Winchester. Although ostensibly a branch line, it was on occasions used as a diversionary route for main line services between London and Bournemouth.

Closed in 1973, the line was reopened between Alresford and Ropley by preservationists in 1977. Titled 'The Watercress Line', the railway currently runs for 10 miles between Alresford and Alton (with a main line connection at the latter).

Ropley station has been developed over the last four decades to become the railway's main engineering headquarters. There is an extensive running shed where locomotive restorations and overhauls are undertaken, together with a wheel-drop facility and separate boiler and carriage workshops. Recent additions to the site include part of the former Kings Cross station footbridge, which connects the north side of the station site with the shed yard.

The station has up and down platforms, providing a passing point for the railway's passenger services, which usually consist of five-coach trains. A variety of motive power has been used over the years, including many types appropriate to the route, such as Maunsell Moguls (classes N and U), Urie S15s, Bulleid Pacifics and T9 No.30120. In recent times A4 Pacific No.60019 Bittern was overhauled for main line use at Ropley and based there for a while between railtour duties. At the time of writing the locomotive roster includes BR Standard Class 4 Mogul No.76017 and Class 9F No.92212, and Ivatt 2MT 2-6-2T No.41312. All these locomotive types are available in OO

Left
Visiting for a gala event, Hughes 2-6-0 No.13065 drifts into Ropley with a down demonstration freight. The adjacent line is a siding, used to store items of stock. To the right is the wall of the boiler shop and carriage works.
Photo: Phil Barnes

as ready-to-run models from either Bachmann or Hornby.

Notes on the plan

The proposed track plan utilises part-relief versions of the large running shed and wheel drop building (at the western side) and the boiler/carriage shed (at the eastern side) to act as visual blocks for the ends of the scenic section. This means that only the ends of the station platforms will need to be modelled. Restricting the scenic section to this part of the station site also keeps the overall length to a very manageable 8'.

The end-to-end scheme would require fiddle yards at each end to enable through running of trains to represent the Alresford to Alton operation. To replicate five-coach trains each of these fiddle yards would need to be around 6' long, but this could be reduced by running shorter formations.

A similar concept has been adopted by Tim Everett, who is constructing an exquisite preservation-era model of Ropley station in 2mm scale. Various models in OO based on the preserved Ropley station have also been constructed over the years.

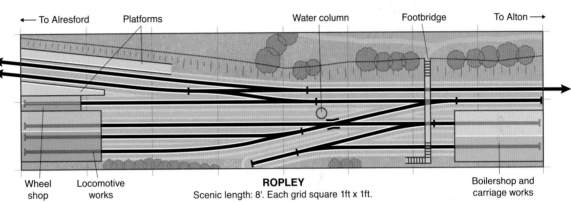

Above

A view from the footplate of an Alton-bound train, looking towards the boiler and coach workshops in the distance. This picture pre-dates the footbridge from which the photo below was taken. Note the modern yard lighting; a small detail that helps to capture a preservation theme in model form.

← To Alresford   Platforms   Water column   Footbridge   To Alton →

Wheel shop   Locomotive works

ROPLEY
Scenic length: 8'. Each grid square 1ft x 1ft.

Boilershop and carriage works

Below

Taken from the restored section of the former Kings Cross footbridge, this December 2013 view shows much of what would be featured on the model as suggested.

Right
Highley station retains much of its original charm. The signal box was used as the basis of the venerable Ratio plastic kit (ref.500).

Highley

PROTOTYPE FEATURE

The Severn Valley Railway

Below
Although the station has just a single platform and passenger trains cannot cross here, much use is made of the loops during special gala events, for freight, light engine and empty stock manoeuvres.

Below
Looking northwards with the running line on the right, seen curving away up Highley bank. Sidings are occupied by permanent way vehicles.

Below right
From the footbridge, showing the former colliery line that now serves the Engine House, which is clearly visible in the distance.

HIGHLEY

Scenic dimensions: 10' x 2'. Each grid square = 1ft x 1ft.

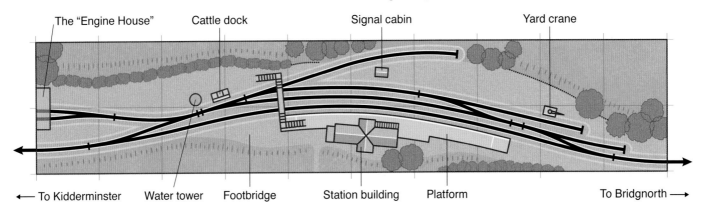

The "Engine House" Cattle dock Signal cabin Yard crane

← To Kidderminster Water tower Footbridge Station building Platform To Bridgnorth →

The prototype described

Highley station was originally a stopping point on the 40-mile Severn Valley route, linking the West Midlands towns of Shrewsbury and Hartlebury. The station was served by a number of nearby collieries, including Alveley colliery – from which freight traffic continued until 1969, six years after the station had closed to passenger traffic.

The preserved Severn Valley Railway (that runs today for 16 miles between Bridgnorth and Kidderminster) ran its first trains to Highley from Bridgnorth in 1974, the station briefly acting as the line's southern terminus until through services to Arley and Bewdley began later in the year.

Highley station has seen significant changes during the preservation era, most notably the construction of The Engine House, which is located immediately to the south of the station site. Opened in 2001 and of modern construction, this extensive visitor centre provides valuable covered accommodation to the railway's locomotives that are out of service awaiting overhaul. However, it presents a stark visual contrast with the surrounding 19th century station architecture. A passenger footbridge was erected in 2009, which is similar to the original one that existed until the early 1970s.

The station building, platforms and signal box (upon which the Ratio ref.500 4mm scale kit is based) are all original features. The cattle dock is a preservation-era construction (based closely on the original), whilst the ex-LNWR water tower was installed during the early 1980s.

Although passenger services cannot pass at Highley (the yard is not signalled for through moves or passenger-carrying trains) the station is often a hive of activity during special events; the yard is often used to enable 'local' passenger sets of two or three coaches (running as empty stock), together with demonstration freights and light engines, to pass with main through passenger workings.

Notes on the plan

Highley station features a distinctive curved formation, which has been retained on the plan, but with the main running straightened out at each end to enable a straight (rather than curving) baseboard footprint to be adopted. The overall length has also been compressed to bring the scenic section down to a more manageable length of 10' in 4mm scale. As such, passenger train lengths can be reduced to five coaches (from the seven or eight that the SVR usually operates on its main services) to suit the reduction in station length. However, fiddle yards at each end to accommodate five-coach trains (plus tender locomotive) would contribute a further 12' to the overall length. The plan incorporates a part-relief representation of the Engine House, which could provide a useful foil for the exit from that end of the scenic section if the layout is configured with viewing side opposite the platform.

Aside from the aforementioned Ratio signal box kit, modelling Highley in 4mm is also assisted with a range of Scenecraft resin buildings for the station that were formerly produced by Bachmann – these can be sourced second-hand. The majority of the locomotive fleet operated by the SVR has also been produced at one time by the ready-to-run manufacturers including Bachmann and Hornby.

Swanage

PROTOTYPE FEATURE

The Swanage Railway

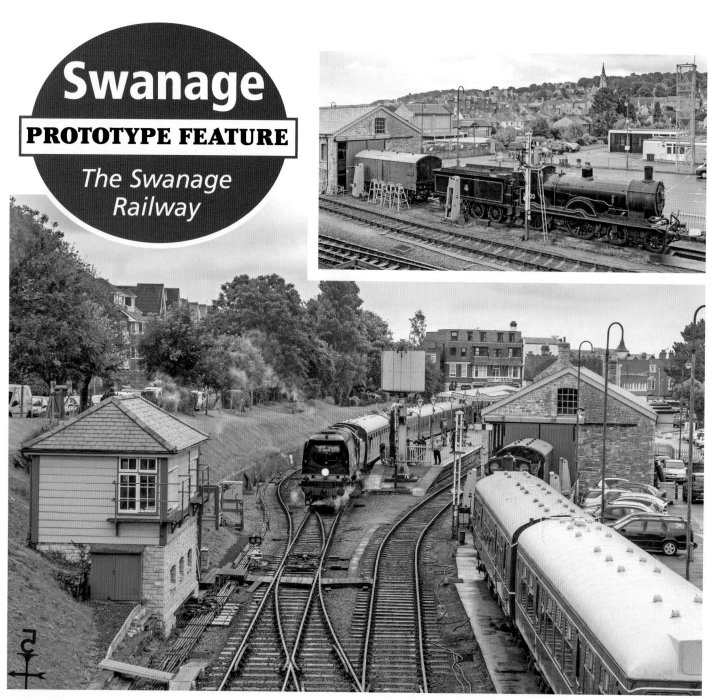

Top
The former goods shed is now used for restoration projects. Beyond is the site of the former goods sidings, now a car park.

Above
A view from the road bridge showing the compact nature of the terminus. The signal box is a convincing modern replica; the original stood on the opposite side of the running lines.

Left
The road bridge with the shed area beyond. Standard 2-6-4Ts have proven to be ideal motive power for the daily services throughout the summer months.

Above
The cramped engine shed area is ripe for replicating in model form. The appearance of double track in this view is deceptive; the lines to the left of the arriving service train are sidings used for stock storage.

Above
The run-round loop can accommodate five coaches. The headshunt is often occupied by various items of stock (such as this ex-BR Type 3), together with a Mk.I coach that serves as a static catering facility for visitors.

The prototype described

Swanage station is the original seaside terminus of the London & South Western Railway's branch from the market town of Wareham. Closed to traffic in 1972, the resurrection of the line – starting from the Swanage terminus – commenced four years later. The first preservation-era trains ran in 1979, with the running line gradually extended in stages until the section through Corfe Castle to Norden was opened in 1995. A connection with the main line was restored in 2002.

Much of the original infrastructure at Swanage station survives, including the canopy, main station building, goods shed and engine shed. However, the LSWR style signal box is a reproduction, situated on the opposite side of the running lines from the original structure.

The original extensive goods yard was swept away long before the line was closed by BR, the former sidings now occupied by a supermarket and parking for buses. The cramped locomotive depot includes a 50' turntable (from Neasdon depot in London, the original having been removed by BR).

Notes on the plan

In difference to the expansive nature of the terminus in the steam era, today's rather more compact station site at Swanage is ideally suited to recreating in model form. The whole site including the shed and turntable area scales out at around 15' in 4mm scale, but a bit of selective compression for the plan drawn has brought this down to

14', which for a portable layout could be configured as four 3'6" boards (measuring 2' deep). The main space saving was undertaken by reducing the platform length, bringing the run-round capacity down from five BR Mk.I coaches to four. However, this still enables a close representation of the railway's service trains to be achieved.

There has been a modicum of modellers' licence used where the running line passes the engine shed; the stock storage line that in reality runs parallel to the main line (on the opposite side from the shed) has been dispensed with, this enabling the main line to exit the scenic section as a single track. A second road bridge has been invented to provide a suitable scenic break.

The turntable includes a short spur for a loco ash wagon; this spur was removed in 2014 but has been retained on the plan to provide a small amount of additional operational interest.

Despite being a compact branch terminus, the railway is home to a number of Bulleid Pacifics – hence the retention of a locomotive release of adequate length. Furthermore, main line charters and gala events have seen Gresley and Stanier Pacifics grace the railway – all of which provide more than enough justification for running equivalent models produced in OO by the likes of Hornby and Bachmann.

Coaching stock is BR Mk.Is for the most-part, together with a couple of Bulleid-designed vehicles and a Devon Belle observation car, which is tagged onto service trains during the peak season. All of these types can be represented in OO with proprietary models.

SWANAGE
Scenic dimensions: 14' x 2'. Each grid square = 1ft x 1ft.

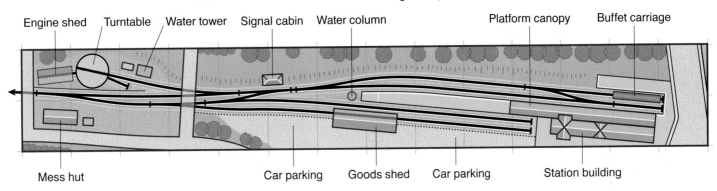

Engine shed   Turntable   Water tower   Signal cabin   Water column   Platform canopy   Buffet carriage

Mess hut   Car parking   Goods shed   Car parking   Station building

Haverthwaite

PROTOTYPE FEATURE

The Lakeside & Haverthwaite Railway

Above
Looking up the line at Haverthwaite from the main platform. The former platform 2 is not used.

Below
The headshunt at Havetherwaite runs into a tunnel; an ideal scenic break on a model. Note the undressed portal that has been cut into the rock.

Above
One of the L&HR's two Fairburn 2-6-4Ts runs round its train at Haverthwaite. (The other is No.42085.) Both have worn lined BR black liveries in recent years.

Below
The rail/boat interchange at Lakeside. The terminus is now without the overall roof pictured on p17. The boat (MV *Teal*) provides leisure cruises on Lake Windermere.

Right
The brick-built Furness Railway-designed signal box at Lakeside dates from 1913. Originally it controlled an extensive three-platform site. *Photo: Steve Flint*

The prototype described

This plan recreates the two surviving stations on the former Windermere Branch of the Furness Railway which was opened throughout in 1869. It originally ran from Ulverston, on the present day Cumbrian Coast line, where it left the main line at a triangular junction at Plumpton. This enabled trains from both eastern and western directions to run to the branch terminus at Lakeside, the small resort at the southern tip of England's largest lake which became an Edwardian tourist destination.

Branch passenger services and excursion traffic were spasmodic during the 20th century due to wartime interruptions and the wayside station at Haverthwaite was closed to passengers in 1947.

Complete closure occurred in 1965 when the entire branch was shut down under the Beeching regime.
Rebirth stumbled through several minor crises until, in 1970, a new company was formed to secure the Haverthwaite to Lakeside section. The tracks back to Plumpton Junction were lifted in 1972 leaving the preserved section cut off completely. Nevertheless the first train under preservation ran on 2 May 1973. The remains of the overall roof at Lakeside were removed fully in 1978 leaving the terminus in the state much as it is today.

The layout plan

Designed as a U-shaped end to end layout, this plan depicts much of the present day infrastructure on the line, albeit sympathetically shortened. It can be built as a permanent home layout if you have a space 12' x 7'7" in which to accommodate it – a large spare room, loft or garage – all viewed and operated from the inside.

However the best views across the model are most likely to be from the outside in an exhibition situation.

It is possible to have three full trains in use and there is just enough head shunt space along the main line section in the tunnel to enable the shunting of each station to be managed without incursion onto the other scene – though two independent operators would have to be in close contact to avoid collisions.

Rolling stock potential

As with any of the schemes in this book, you as the builder could run whatever takes your fancy, but to be truly authentic, loco classes on this railway will be limited to that which the railway currently has in its roster. These are notably the original pair of Fairburn 2-6-4Ts, together with a number of 0-6-0 and 0-4-0 industrial tanks. Several diesel locos are in the collection including a Class 20, Class 26 and a 'Calder Valley' Class 110 DMU set. Coaching stock is restricted to trusty BR Mk.I carriages (one converted for disabled access with end observation windows fitted), with virtually no freight whatsoever, except for permanent way duties and use on special photo charters.

In other words, as with all railway modelling, being a thorough purist can be limiting to what you should be running, but let your imagination run wild a little, and this layout can play host to whatever you like – all in a beautiful lakeland setting.

Above
Bagnall *Victor* – sister to *Vulcan* (see p18), in steam at Haverthwaite.
Photos on this page and opposite by Dave Enefer except where stated

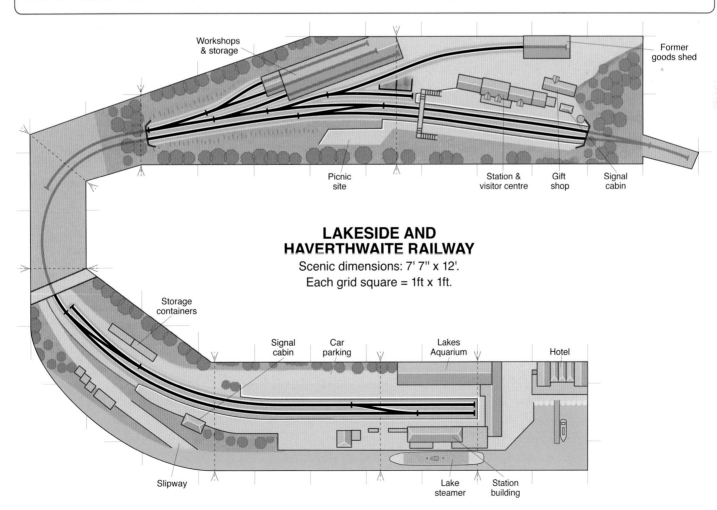

Workshops & storage

Former goods shed

Picnic site

Station & visitor centre

Gift shop

Signal cabin

Storage containers

Signal cabin

Car parking

Lakes Aquarium

Hotel

Slipway

Lake steamer

Station building

LAKESIDE AND HAVERTHWAITE RAILWAY
Scenic dimensions: 7' 7" x 12'.
Each grid square = 1ft x 1ft.

Ingrow & Oakworth

PROTOTYPE FEATURE

Keighley & Worth Valley Railway

Right
Stanier Class 5MT No.45212 arrives at Ingrow, having emerged from the tunnel situated at the end of the platform. The site's proximity to roads and housing can be clearly seen. The station building is a rebuilt structure recovered from Foulridge.
All photos this page: Derek Shore

Left
Looking towards the Engine Shed at Ingrow (originally the station's goods shed) located in the yard, with the running line on the left. The double-slip would prove to be a useful space saver in model form.

Top
A roadside view of Ingrow station. A selection of modern vehicles would help to define a layout as a preservation depiction. Note the different lamp designs.

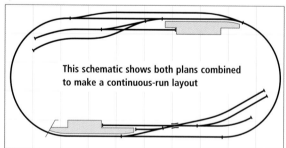

This schematic shows both plans combined to make a continuous-run layout

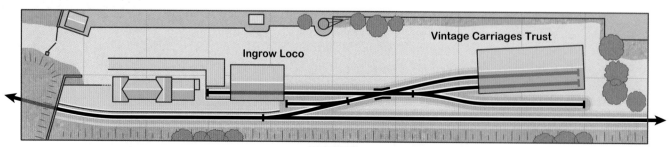

Ingrow Loco

Vintage Carriages Trust

INGROW
Overall size: 10' x 2'. Each grid square 1ft x 1ft.

Above
The extensive Vintage Carriages Trust building at Ingrow, which has been constructed in a modern style, which contrasts with the surviving station architecture.
Photo: Derek Shore

Above right
A steam crane in action in Oakworth yard, where permanent way vehicles and equipment are stored. The running line can be seen to the right of the picture.
Photo: Alan Padley

Right
The route of the original loop line can be made out in this view of Oakworth, which featured in the 1970 film *The Railway Children*.
Photo: Dave Enefer

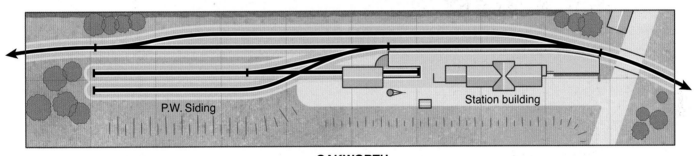

P.W. Siding

Station building

OAKWORTH
Overall size: 10' x 2'. Each grid square 1ft x 1ft.

The prototype described

The Worth Valley branch line out of Keighley was originally opened in 1867, having been funded predominantly by local mill owners. It was soon absorbed into the Midland Railway and ran successfully for many years until road competition resulted in its closure in 1962. Local opposition to closure saw the inauguration of the Keighley and Worth Valley Railway Preservation Society and as a result of its efforts the line reopened to the public in 1968.

Notes on the plans

Any of the stations on this railway are all worthy of modelling, but two of the intermediate stops have been selected. Of the pair, Oakworth has to be the most famous, immortalised in the original 1970s movie The Railway Children in which the curmudgeonly station porter, Mr Perks, was played by Bernard Cribbins.

Oakworth was provided with a goods loop for many years, but it was lifted in 1956 and never reinstated. However for operational variety we suppose it was retained, though not for passenger trains, rather for the occasional photographic 'goods' special train, or permanent way trains. In fact the old goods yard is a storage area for such vehicles and materials, enabling PW workings in and out of the

sidings to further increase interest and operating potential.

The not so famous Ingrow Station, being further down the valley and closer to industrial Keighley, sits amid more urban surroundings. A short tunnel immediately at the western end of the station platform is a real example of the sort of scenic break much loved by modellers short on space. The original station building had to be demolished shortly after reopening to the public. The structure which occupies the site today is a tasteful relocation and rebuild of the one which previously stood at Foulridge on the Skipton to Colne line.

The former goods yard is now the home of RAIL STORY; two museums dedicated to rail travel. The Vintage Carriage Trust occupies the twin track display area and workshop, which in model form could offer some further operational interest with passenger vehicles shunted to and fro. The Bahamas Locomotive Society operates the second museum in the old goods shed – Ingrow Loco – which also houses several locos under the custodianship of the Society. Further operational interest exists with the occasional exchange of locos.

Either plan would be suitable for an end-to-end scheme in its own right, but with modification they can be combined into one single continuous run layout as shown in the schematic plan opposite.

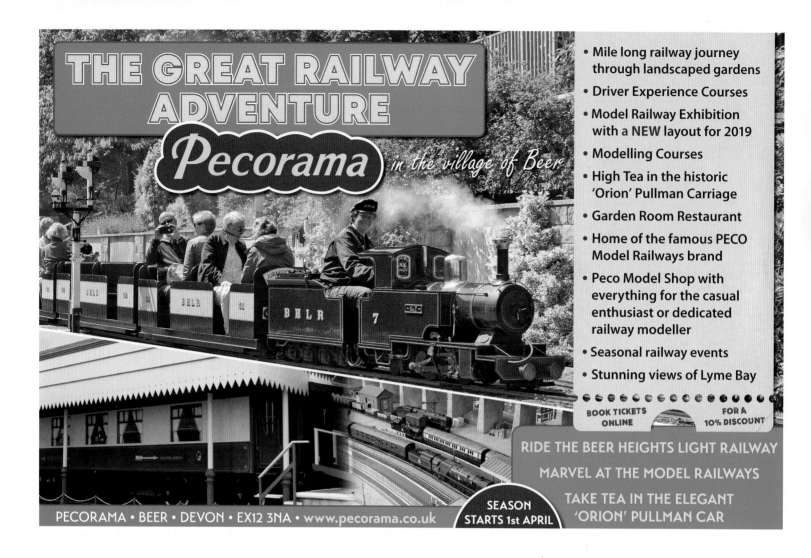
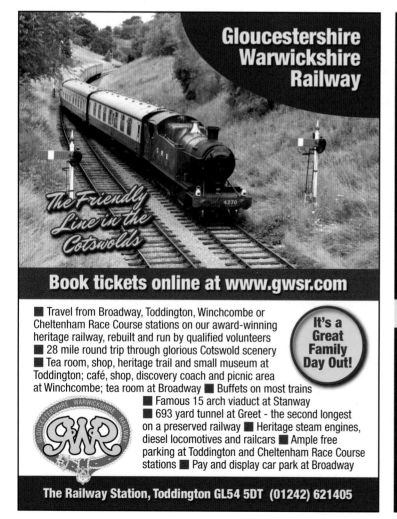

Chapter 3

Railway centres and museums

Whereas heritage railways tend to focus their efforts towards providing visitors with the experience of rail travel, with a train journey being the primary attraction, railway centres and museums serve first and foremost to preserve collections of locomotives and stock, together with railway structures, infrastructure and artefacts.

This differentiation between heritage lines and railway centres/museums isn't, however, always quite that clear cut; many heritage railways incorporate museums as part of their additional attractions (such as the Engine House on the Severn Valley Railway), whilst many museums have running lines that provide train rides to augment their static displays of exhibits (such as Locomotion at Shildon). Furthermore, there are examples of museum running lines that are in fact longer than some heritage railways (such as the Midland Railway – Butterley, which boasts a 3½ mile running line).

Muddying the waters of this differentiation still further, this chapter includes plans for schemes that could be categorised as heritage railways – these being the plans for Washford station on the West Somerset Railway, and the Ribble Steam Railway. However, the Washford plan is centred around the museum site and satellite operations of the Somerset & Dorset Railway Trust, with the operation of the heritage railway serving the station being a secondary function. And, whilst

the Ribble Steam Railway offers a return trip of more than three miles, passengers can only board and alight trains at Preston Riverside, and the *raison d'être* for the preservation scheme is the preservation of an extensive collection of industrial locomotives, which occupies a museum building located alongside the platform.

Museums in model form

On the face of it, museums of static exhibits could appear to offer little in the way of modelling potential for those seeking to build a working layout. However, a museum space can be included as a scenic feature as part of a larger layout scheme, such as what Robin Brogden achieved with his *Museum of Transport* model. Similarly, the Locomotion plan presented in this chapter also has the potential for modelling part of the interior museum space, and replicating a portion of the static exhibits displayed therein.

The appeal of modelling a museum of static exhibits as part of a layout is that there are no restrictions on the models you can include; early 19th century steam locomotives like Stephenson's *Rocket* can be displayed alongside mid-20th century designs such No.92220 *Evening Star*, electric locomotives can be featured without the need to provide overhead live equipment (OHLE), and London

Right
Robin Brogden has modelled an exhibition hall as part of his extensive 4mm scale *Museum of Transport* layout, which has enabled a wide variety of rail vehicles to be displayed alongside each other. Note how models of smaller scales have been used to represent miniature locomotives.
Photo: Robin Brogden

Below
Although the Severn Valley Railway is first and foremost a 16-mile heritage railway, it also has this impressive locomotive display building and exhibition space at the line's Highley station.

Bottom right
The Great Hall at York's Railway Museum. The yard outside features a demonstration line and miniature railway.

Underground vehicles could be placed – perhaps incongruously – alongside a model of APT-E! And why restrict the choice of models to those of British outline? Many UK museum collections include railway exhibits from overseas, which provides ample justification for assembling a truly eclectic mix of exhibits for a museum in model form.

Large locos, short trains and compact spaces

As was stated in Chapter 1, railway centres pioneered much of the preservation movement in the UK, these being established at locations such as Dinting, Carnforth, Tyseley and Didcot; all of these examples occupying former steam motive power depots that had become vacant following the displacement of steam traction on British Railways. The attraction of these sites to the fledgling preservation groups was clear to see – the former running sheds provided ideal covered storage for preserved loco-

motives and stock, whilst rail connections to the national network were already in place.

From a modelling perspective, the attraction of a railway centre scheme based around a locomotive depot is that these sites can be quite compact in nature, making them well-suited to those looking to house a fulfilling layout scheme in a modest available space. Furthermore, a railway centre scheme also shares similar opportunities to the traditional steam/diesel depot layout, in that models of large locomotive types can be operated 'light engine' in a plausible environment, thereby negating any need to have space for lengthy express passenger train formations or long rakes of freight vehicles.

However, whereas a traditional depot layout rarely has any operational scope over and above the running of light engines, a preservation scheme does create opportunities for passenger shuttles to be included, such as those operated at Shildon and Didcot. At Shildon just a single brake van is employed (adapted for passenger use), whilst at Didcot, the main demonstration line typically comprises just two coaches. At both of these locations large locomotives have been used on these duties, such as Gresley Pacifics, Collett Kings and Deltics.

A mix of gauges

For further modelling variety, there are numerous railway centres that feature a mix of gauges, with miniature railways and narrow gauge lines situated alongside the standard gauge systems. The Midland Railway – Butterley is a good example, where the 2' gauge Golden Valley Light Railway has been developed, whilst miniature railways can

Above
Barrow Hill Roundhouse operates passenger rides alongside the extensive shed yard.

Left
A contrast of old and new at Manchester's Museum of Science & Industry with replica locomotive *Planet* alongside the site's modernised architecture.
Photo: Phil Barnes

Below left
Displayed inside MOSI is this Gorton-built former EM2 in Netherlands Railways livery.
Photo: Phil Barnes

Below
A view of the very short platform constructed at MOSI for passenger rides.
Photo: Phil Barnes

Right
Super power at Didcot with a pair of King 4-6-0s (Nos.6023 and 6024) hauling just two coaches on the railway centre's short demonstration line, which proves that you don't need lots of space or long train formations to utilise models of big locomotives.

be found as part of the visitor attractions at Yeovil Railway Centre and York's Railway Museum.

Representing what is perhaps the ultimate in mixed gauges exists at Didcot Railway Centre, where a broad gauge demonstration line has been constructed, complete with a dual-gauge section that integrates with the standard gauge branch demonstration line.

Below & right
Occupying a relatively small area of land that wasn't originally of railway use, Bressingham Steam Gardens features standard, narrow and miniature gauge running lines.
Photos: Colour Rail (below) and Kieran Hardy (right)

Above & left
The Buckinghamshire Railway Centre has established a collection of vehicles and relocated buildings at Quainton Road. The centre's operational arrangement is unique, its site being split by the (unconnected) freight-only line that runs through the station. *Photo (left): Phil Barnes*

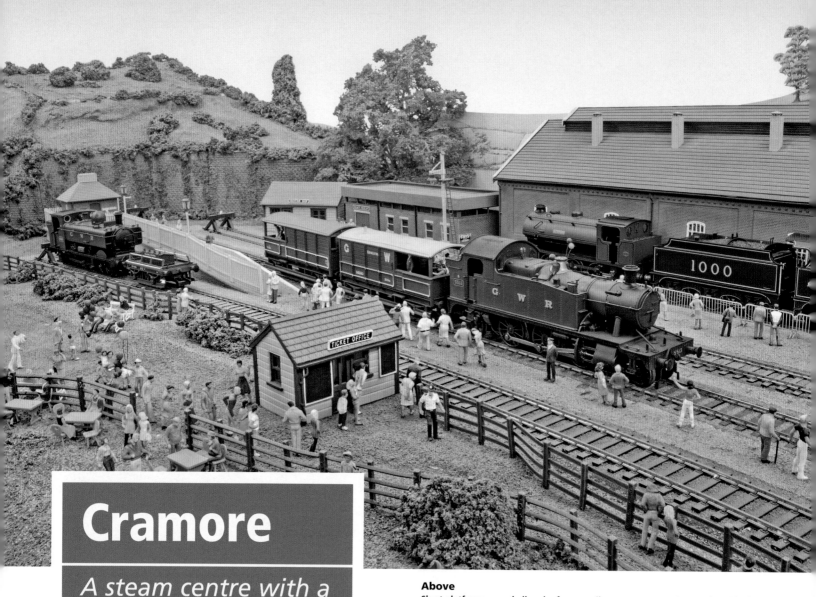

Cramore

A steam centre with a main line connection

Constructed in OO by Pecorama modelmakers

A former exhibit in the Pecorama model railway exhibition, Cramore was constructed to show visitors how they could 'cram more' into a space measuring slightly less than 9' x 8' whilst maintaining plenty of operating potential. A theme of a contemporary steam centre was adopted to allow a collection of preserved locomotives to be displayed alongside examples of modern traction operating services on the 'main line'. It was supposed that a preservation society had acquired the redundant shed area from BR, in a similar way to the Great Western Society's headquarters at Didcot and the former 'Steamtown' attraction at Carnforth.

Aspects were also derived from the East Somerset Railway, which has its main terminus at Cranmore – the shed on the layout was in fact based on the brick-built structure at Cranmore, which was constructed early in the railway's preservation era under the tenure of its late founder, David Shepherd. There is also a modern workshop built using the Peco Train Shed Unit kit (LK-80), where it is presumed that restoration and repair work is undertaken.

The steam centre is linked to the main line station via a footpath and footbridge. The layout is well-populated with figures, which evokes the atmosphere of a busy open day.

Notes on the plan

In its original Pecorama context the lines entering tunnels on the plan (which was the last one devised for the exhibition by Peco Founder Sydney Pritchard) connected with an adjoining layout to allow for

through running of trains and visiting main line specials. However, following the subsequent rebuilding of this adjoining layout, the operation on Cramore was restricted to a DMU shuttle along the section between the station and a hidden storage line just through the lower tunnel mouth.

The plan offers plenty of potential as the basis of a self-contained scheme in the home – the main line section could be modified quite easily to allow for continuous running, together with the inclusion of hidden storage sidings. Aside from the main line operation, the layout featured a brake van shuttle that operated within the confines of the steam centre. Similar types of shuttle operation are still employed at railway centres around the country, including Locomotion at Shildon.

A particular feature of the layout is the clever use of curved track, which was a preference of Sydney's; the minimum track radius was not less than 18". Being a circular design brought the advantage of creating an illusion of distance for the operator; positioned in the central well at the controls of the layout, it was not possible to see all sides at the same time, therefore giving the illusion of trains running out of sight and into the distance.

Furthermore, the sharpest curves are situated on the section of track that forms the railway centre's demonstration line and, by utilising four-wheel brake vans for carrying passengers – rather than lengthy bogie coaches – the visual severity of the radii can be disguised.

Below
A busy day at Cramore, which evokes the atmosphere of open days at railway centres around the country, such as Didcot and Barrow Hill.

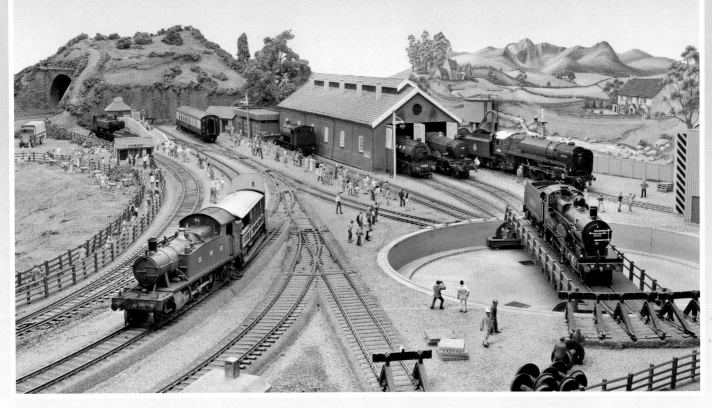

Below
Despite being part of the national network, the station retains much of its steam-era architecture. The running in boards on the platform further reinforce the preservation theme of the layout.

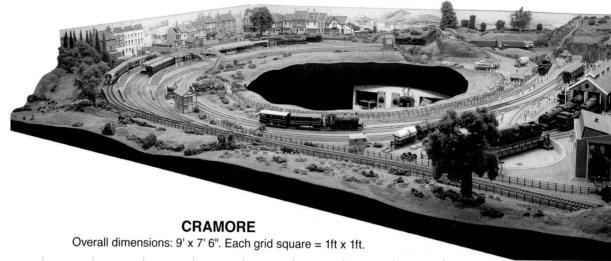

Right
An overall view of the
layout showing the central
operating well.

CRAMORE
Overall dimensions: 9' x 7' 6". Each grid square = 1ft x 1ft.

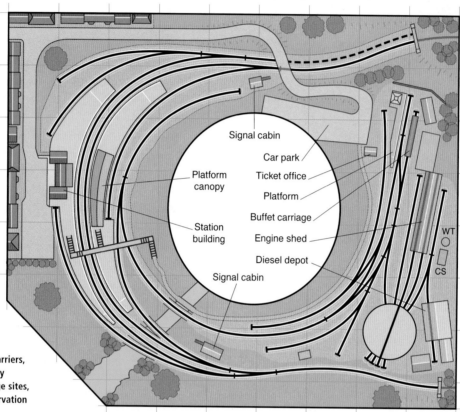

Signal cabin

Car park

Ticket office

Platform
canopy

Platform

Buffet carriage

Station
building

Engine shed

Diesel depot

Signal cabin

WT

CS

Below
Small details such as these
modern-style pedestrian barriers,
which are a feature of many
railway centres and heritage sites,
help to reinforce the preservation
theme of the model.

Above
Contemporary main line services on the layout are augmented with Class 158s, an example of which is seen here. Much of the scenic work can be undertaken using traditional layout building materials and techniques.

Below
A Hunslet Austerity 0-6-0ST is seen at the end of the railway centre's demonstration line with a brake van passenger shuttle.

Locomotion

PROTOTYPE FEATURE

Railway Museum at Shildon

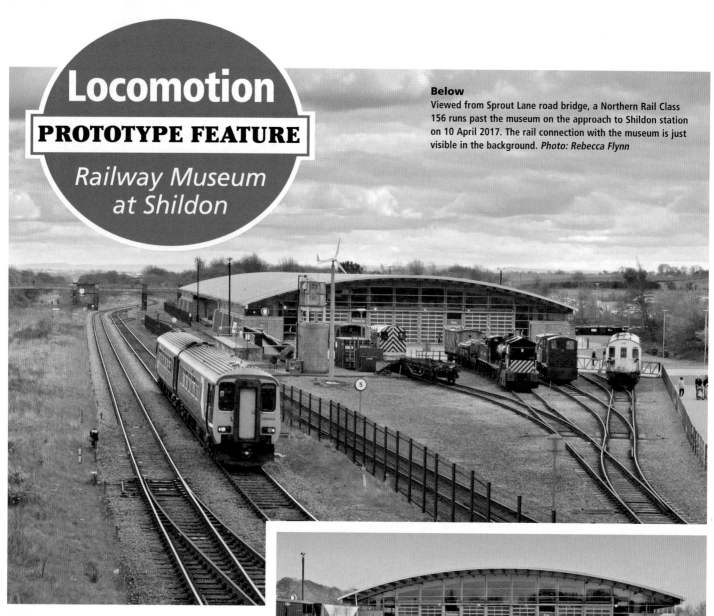

Right
The museum's impressive frontage, with a preserved LMS brake van and HAA hopper parked outside. Extensive use is made of inset track: see RM January 2012.
Photo: Rebecca Flynn

The prototype described

As far as visual contrasts go, there is not much that can rival the stark juxtaposition of elegant Victorian steam locomotives displayed outside the bold and modern outline of the museum structure at Shildon, completed in 2004.

An annexe of the Railway Museum at York, Locomotion primarily houses locomotives, rolling stock and other exhibits that belong to the National Collection. The museum is located alongside the Tees Valley Line that runs between Bishop Auckland and Darlington. There is a main line connection with the museum site, which is used to exchange exhibits between York and Shildon, and also to receive main line locomotives for special events.

The museum site also features a 1km running line, which is operated as a passenger shuttle with a specially adapted BR 20T brakevan. Small industrial locomotive types are the usual motive power, but special events have seen larger locomotives (including A4 Pacifics!) performing these duties.

Notes on the plan

The museum structure is huge and would be impractical to model in full. Therefore, only part of the structure has been suggested; the full front elevation and a sufficient section of its length (about 18") to enable it to act as a visual block for the main line that runs off the scenic section behind. This would also allow some items of stock to be

displayed inside if desired, together with a representation of the interior detail. Sprout Lane road bridge provides an ideal scenic break at the other end of the model.

The apron outside the front of the museum is used to display exhibits for special events, and this would be a key feature of the layout – it providing an ideal setting for modellers who own examples from the National Collection In Miniature range marketed by Locomotionmodels.com (including the prototype Deltic, Great Northern Atlantic No.251 and the Stirling Single).

Similarly, the museum's 'Great Goodbye' event of February 2014 could be faithfully recreated using the Hornby set of all six preserved Gresley A4 Pacifics.

The plan is drawn to scale, with only the representation of the main line connection deviating from the actual configuration; in reality this connection is situated at the other end of the museum building, but it adds to the operational scope of the layout to have this included 'on scene'.

The main line operation is largely confined to two-car DMUs, for which short fiddle yards could be used at each end. Operation of this could even be controlled by an automated shuttle. The museum passenger shuttle could be operated using a single brake van (adapted from the venerable Airfix/Dapol plastic kit or Bachmann model), together with almost any preserved locomotive of your choosing.

Below
A line up of East Coast Main Line motive power on display outside the museum in 2016; Deltic No.D9002 *The King's Own Yorkshire Light Infantry*, A4 No.60009 *Union of South Africa* and A3 No.60103 *Flying Scotsman. Photo: Martin Creese*

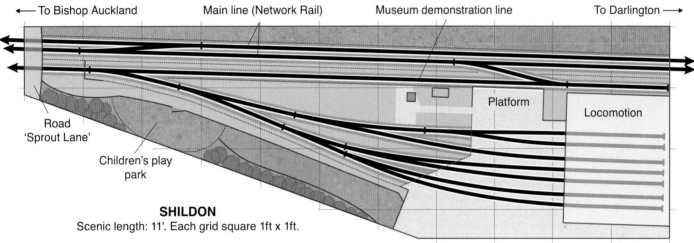

← To Bishop Auckland   Main line (Network Rail)   Museum demonstration line   To Darlington →

Road 'Sprout Lane'

Children's play park

Platform

Locomotion

SHILDON
Scenic length: 11'. Each grid square 1ft x 1ft.

Below
Looking from the museum apron towards Sprout Lane bridge. Note the level crossing gates to allow for shared road/rail access. The fencing divides the museum from the main line. *Photo: Rebecca Flynn*

Above
Photographed from the short platform just outside the entrance to the museum building (with the main line visible behind), Robert Heath & Sons Ltd 0-4-0ST No.6 (built 1885) is being used for rides along the demonstration line in this August 2006 view. Note the former BR 20T brakevan – with specially converted verandahs – being used to provide passenger accommodation.

Rowley Station

PROTOTYPE FEATURE

Beamish Museum

Below
The 1900s Town area of the museum site – complete with trams – is situated adjacent to Rowley station and could form an interesting scenic cameo, as suggested on the accompanying plan.

Above
Andrew Barclay 0-4-0ST No.22 performs shunting demonstrations in this August 2006 view. The station building is visible behind. The trees in the background provide an ideal visual foil to run along the back of a layout.

The prototype described

Rowley station and its short passenger line forms one of the parts of the extensive museum site at Beamish, the North of England Open Air Museum in County Durham. The compact station site was developed in the 1970s to demonstrate a 'typical' small passenger and goods facility as operated by the North Eastern Railway.

The site includes a mix of original and relocated structures from around the north-east; the station building was originally from nearby Rowley, the 1896-built signal box from Carr House near Consett, the goods shed from Alnwick, the coal drop from West Boldon, the weighbridge from Glanton and the coal office from Hexham.

At one end of the site is a large corrugated building with the wording 'Beamish Waggon and Iron Works, est.1857' – this is a regional museums store but includes two covered sidings that house the locomotives and passenger stock used on the railway.

The running line extends for a short distance away from the station (less than ¼ mile) – which means that conceivably a 4mm model of the entire setup could be created without any compression!

Train operations consist of wagon shunting demonstrations in the station yard and a passenger shuttle out and back along the running line. Locomotives tend to be small industrial designs, whilst former NER/LNER classes have been used on occasions – including the sole-surviving Y7 0-4-0T.

Peripheral features that would add particular interest to such a model are the adjacent town with tramway, and fairground, in the field alongside the goods sidings.

Notes on the plan

The regional museum store building provides an ideal scenic block for one end of the scenic section, which has been suggested as part-relief, with sufficient depth to accommodate a loco or short coach inside on one of the covered sidings. The station layout has been drawn to scale, athough the siding serving the coal drops has been shortened to keep the depth of the scenic section sensible.

The end of the running line is hidden behind the row of town

cottages, which themselves have been moved closer to the station site. The section of tramway (which could be modelled as a static feature) has similarly been moved across with the cottages, bringing this slightly closer to the station site than is the case in reality.

The layout could be self-contained, as per the prototype, although connecting the running line to a short fiddle yard, or even a portable cassette, could be considered to provide additional variety for the stock used.

Short passenger coaches – particularly of North Eastern design – are not readily available as ready-to-run items, but a Ratio GWR four-wheel coach kit could be used to deputise as a vehicle of broadly similar outline and length.

Proprietary models of motive power in keeping with that used by the museum could include the Bachmann J72 0-6-0T, Hornby Peckett 0-4-0ST or Dapol/Hornby/DJ Models J94 0-6-0ST.

Below
A cameo recorded from the station building, which illustrates the level of detail the museum has incorporated into the rebuilt station scene.

Right
The sidings around the station site are occupied by various items of rolling stock, including a number of former North Eastern Railway vehicles. This view was taken from the footbridge at the western end of the site.

Below
Vulcan Foundry-built 0-4-0ST *Vulcan* is pictured whilst being serviced outside the regional museum store, coupled to the single four-wheel coach used for passenger rides.
Photo: Steve Flint

Right
Taken from the footbridge at the eastern end of the station site, this view encompasses almost the entire track layout, with just the short running line extending behind the camera position.

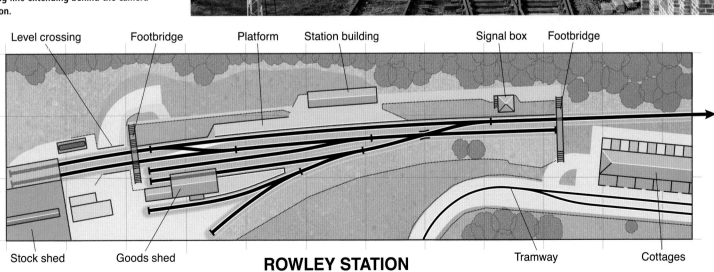

Level crossing   Footbridge   Platform   Station building   Signal box   Footbridge

Stock shed   Goods shed   Tramway   Cottages

ROWLEY STATION
Scenic dimensions: 11' x 6'. Each grid square = 1ft x 1ft.

Washford

PROTOTYPE FEATURE

The West Somerset Railway

Below
Visiting 57xx 0-6-0PT No.7714 arrives at Washford with a WSR service train for Minehead, whilst the S&DRT's 0-4-0ST *Kilmersdon* (in pseudo lined S&DJR Prussian blue) is engaged in shunting duties around the adjacent museum site.

Above
These grounded van and coach bodies would form an interesting scenic cameo on a layout based on the Washford station site, for which the respective Ratio plastic kits could be used.

Above
The S&DR Trust possesses an assortment of freight vehicles, many of which have been beautifully restored, with others stored awaiting their turn in the workshops. Note those covered in protective tarpaulins, which could form the basis of another interesting cameo.

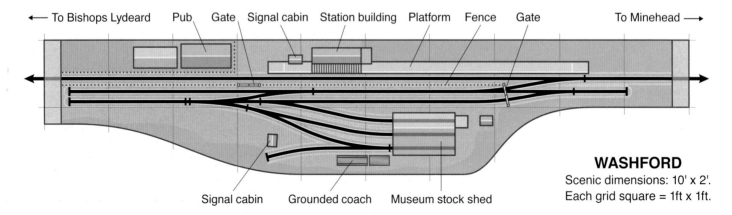

← To Bishops Lydeard   Pub   Gate   Signal cabin   Station building   Platform   Fence   Gate   To Minehead →

Signal cabin   Grounded coach   Museum stock shed

WASHFORD
Scenic dimensions: 10' x 2'.
Each grid square = 1ft x 1ft.

The prototype described

Washford is an intermediate station on the West Somerset Railway, which runs for nearly 23 miles from Bishops Lydeard to the seaside terminus at Minehead. The former GWR branch line originally connected to the main line at Taunton; this section of line is still extant and occasionally is used to bring railtours and main line-certified locomotives to and from the preserved railway. The branch closed on 4 January 1971, with the embryonic preservation scheme (incorporated as the West Somerset Railway Co.) commencing its services from Minehead in March 1976, thereafter re-opening the route in stages to Bishops Lydeard.

Washford has never served as a passing point for passenger services, it always having just the single platform. The station originally featured a goods loop and associated sidings, together with a goods shed and cattle dock. However, these structures were demolished soon after goods services ceased in 1964.

Since 1975 the Somerset & Dorset Railway Trust has been based in the former goods yard at Washford, which has acquired a vast collection of S&D artefacts. In 1989 the workshop was erected, which houses some of the Trust's locomotives and items of rolling stock.

On some days when the WSR is running services the trust operates shunting demonstrations within the confines of its Washford site, using its industrial 0-4-0STs and small diesel shunter locomotives. However, it is understood that movements between the main running line and the yard are not ordinarily undertaken during timetabled WSR operation.

Notes on the plan

In terms of the main WSR running line, Washford station has limited operational scope for the modeller, but the Trust's yard operations provide plenty of opportunities for shuffling handfuls of wagons around using small industrial types – such as the Hornby Peckett 0-4-0ST. Furthermore, the trust's eclectic mix of rolling stock would make for an interesting collection to assemble in model form.

Furthermore, there's no reason why a small amount of modellers' licence couldn't be used to have further interaction between the yard and the main line, with short demonstration freights running to and from the yard.

The WSR has hosted a wide array of locomotive types over the years to operate its services, including large express passenger steam locomotives from the Big Four, DMUs, diesel hydraulics and even HSTs! Loco-hauled passenger trains are typically formed of six BR Mk.I coaches.

The Washford site is already a compact prototype, but the plan has been compressed to bring the scenic length down to 10', by using smaller radius pointwork in the yard and by shortening the two sidings at the Bishops Lydeard end. Some simplification of the pointwork may be desirable, particularly the pair of interlaced two-way points that form the connection with the WSR running line. It is envisaged that the plan could form part of a larger system, such as a continuous run around a room, perhaps with a larger station on the opposite side (such as Williton).

Above
Various signs of modern times (such as the 'portaloos', yard lighting and Vauxhall Vectra) mark this out as a 21st century scene, with these items contrasting with the recovered Burnham-on-Sea signal cabin, SR-type box van and Ruston 88DS diesel shunter.

Below
This view clearly illustrates how the S&DRT site is segregated from the WSR running line with gated access points and fencing. A broad representation of the station building could be achieved by adapting the Peco 'Manyways' stone country station kit (ref.LK-13).

Above
Access between the WSR running line and the museum yard is via this gated crossover. The points are controlled by a ground frame, unlocked by a key in a train staff issued by either Blue Anchor or Williton signal boxes.

Preston Riverside
PROTOTYPE FEATURE
The Ribble Steam Railway

Below
Former NCB Scottish Area Bowhill Coal Preparation Plant 'No.6' (Andrew Barclay 0-4-0ST, works No.2261 – built in 1949) heads back to Preston Riverside from Strand Road across the Riversway swing bridge on 13 September 2014.
Photo: Gordon Edgar

The prototype described

A relative newcomer to the ranks of heritage lines in the UK, the Ribble Steam Railway opened to the public in 2005. It occupies part of the once extensive industrial rail network around Preston Docks. The railway is home to a large collection of industrial locomotives, much of which was relocated to Preston in 1999 from the defunct Southport Railway Museum (Steamport). The railway is also the base of the Furness Railway Trust and its collection of locomotives.

Weekend passenger operations are typically composed of a single rake of three BR Mk.I coaches, hauled by a small industrial steam locomotive or diesel. From the main operational base at Preston Riverside, the three-mile return trip includes crossing the dock swing bridge (a unique feature on a UK heritage railway) and then along the bank of the River Ribble to Strand Road. There is no run-round or station facilities here, so trains are propelled back to the exchange sidings where running round can be undertaken; the gangway of the end coach has been adapted for this purpose (see p120).

A separate company, Ribble Rail, operates freight traffic during the week that runs over the RSR route, bringing in bitumen for the Total plant sited near Riverside station. The bitumen tankers arrive (hauled by a Class 60 or 66) via a connecting line that runs between Strand Road and the WCML at Preston main line station. From the exchange sidings, the tankers are taken to Riverside by a Sentinel diesel shunter (from the RSR fleet), before being propelled along the Lafina Road siding for discharging. The reverse procedure is undertaken with the empty tankers.

Notes on the plan

The Ribble Steam Railway offers tremendous operational potential, particularly if the heritage passenger workings were to be interlaced with the bitumen traffic, thus presenting the enticing prospect of industrial steam locomotives rubbing shoulders with modern main line diesels. There are plenty of contrasts between old and new with the scenery too, with modern housing estates and industrial buildings neighbouring the railway, all providing an unlikely backdrop for the heritage locomotives and rolling stock.

The suggested plan is a complete reinterpretation of the RSR system, which incorporates all the elements needed to replicate the aforementioned operations, but with signifcant compression and changes to configure it for the 11' x 8' format to occupy a spare room. The shortened loops could accommodate a rake of three TEAs (replaced by ICA-G bitumen bogie tankers in 2010), but smaller four-wheel tankers may better suit – visually at least – the radii of the curves and pointwork used.

The plan includes a short demountable (or hinged) section at the end of Riverside station to allow for the doorway. The hidden siding could take the form of a lift-out cassette. The plan includes a supposed platform at the Strand Road end of the passenger operation, as per the eventual aims of the RSR.

Below
Colas Rail Freight 60095 crosses Strand Road in order to gain access to the exchange sidings with the 6M32 loaded bitumen from Lindsey Refinery on 17 June 2015. *Photo: Gordon Edgar*

Left
The gated entrance to the Lafina siding, with the end of a rake of VTG bogie tankers just discernible, together with the apparatus used to discharge the bitumen for the Total plant. The curvature of the siding necessitates the fitting of a check rail along the inside.

Above
Preston Riverside station, with the museum building on the left and a Sentinel shunter exchanging rakes of bitumen tankers. The railbus was on loan to the RSR and engaged on passenger services.
Both photos: David Enefer

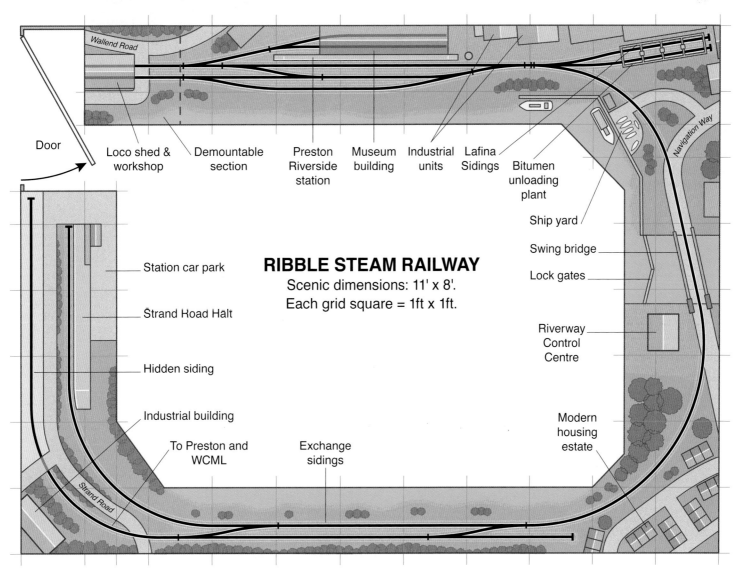

Wallend Road

Door

Loco shed & workshop

Demountable section

Preston Riverside station

Museum building

Industrial units

Lafina Sidings

Bitumen unloading plant

Navigation Way

Ship yard

Swing bridge

Lock gates

Station car park

Strand Hoad Halt

Hidden siding

Industrial building

To Preston and WCML

Exchange sidings

Strand Road

Riverway Control Centre

Modern housing estate

RIBBLE STEAM RAILWAY
Scenic dimensions: 11' x 8'.
Each grid square = 1ft x 1ft.

M Shed

PROTOTYPE FEATURE

The Bristol Harbour Railway

Left
The passenger platform at Princes Wharf, which is just long enough to accommodate the short rake of vehicles used, which includes a Toad brake van.

Above
The modernised dockside structures of M Shed contrasts with the BHR stock. A preserved tug (1935-built *John King*) is seen on the left moored to the dockside.

Below
A train returns to the station at Princes Wharf, which is located alongside M Shed (the building on the right). The passenger vehicles comprise a coverted Conflat (nearest the locomotive) and a Turbot bogie ballast wagon.

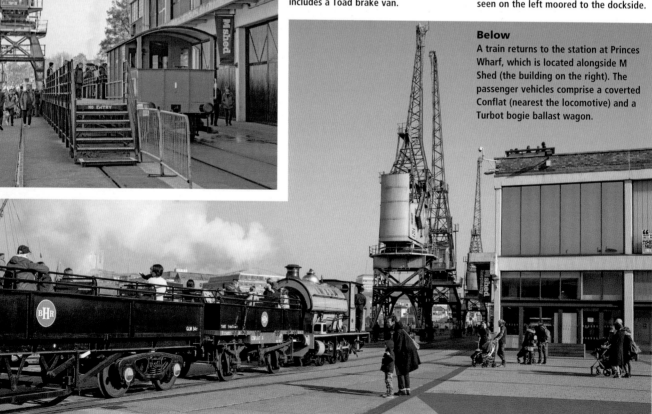

The prototype described

Opened in 1849 by the Eastern Union Railway, and situated 3½ miles from the junction with the Liverpool Street to Norwich main line, Chappel & Wakes Colne station is the first stop on the single track branch line from Marks Tey to Sudbury. This line, now known as the 'Gainsborough Line' (after local painter Thomas Gainsborough who was born in Sudbury) is a remarkable survivor given the very rural nature of this part of Essex. Indeed, under the Beeching Report the whole of the 46½-mile line from Marks Tey to Cambridge was scheduled for closure. However the 11¾-mile section from Marks Tey to Sudbury was reprieved.

The station may be unstaffed for regular services, but there is a lot of activity and interest around the station site. Virtually everything here survives divided between 'museum pieces' and active buildings operated by EARM staff.

In the approach road to the station there is a plinthed 0-4-0ST, No.2039 Jeffrey. It was built by Peckett & Sons in 1943 and last worked at the Glenwydd Ironworks Foundry, Shropshire. The loco was transferred to Chappel in 1981.

There are three platforms – platform 1 for National Rail, platform 2 for longer EARM rides and platform 3 by the restoration shed for abbreviated brakevan rides to and from the goods shed.

Below platform 1, which is perched on a lofty embankment high above the approach road, there are souvenir and book shops, both operated by the EARM. To reach the museum from platform 1 involves a complex route crossing the footbridge onto platform 2 and then through the two pairs of level crossing gates into the yard. (This can be a lengthy process as the gates have to be locked and unlocked every time a rail movement passes.) Here may be found the restoration shed and the small platform 3 alongside from where short brakevan rides are offered.

At the south end of the EARM site is Chappel South signal box which is more akin to a small covered ground frame. Further up is a miniature railway, then comes the substantial stone-built goods shed. One track enters the shed from the north so that exhibits may be put under cover.

Chappel North signal box on platform 3 controls all movements around the yard and is fully operational with a splendid array of working semaphore arm and ground disc signals.

The EARM site has a pretty complex array of tracks squeezed into a narrow site. At the south end there are two headshunts each long enough to take a loco and not much more. The outer headshunt (as you look north) feeds a loop line which leads to the restoration shed and coal bunker and four dead-end tracks to the rear of the goods shed. The inner headshunt only accesses platform 2 and the loop line around the back of this platform.

Platform 2, the loops and the goods shed dovetail into the north end headshunt that abuts Spring Lane overbridge. The overbridge effectively delineates the extent of the EARM site. It is into this headshunt that brakevan rides and driver experience runs are routed.

(Abridged from an article by Myles Munsey, published in RAILWAY MODELLER January 2015.)

Top
Jubilee taking water prior to another run along the site. The tank in the background would make a good first kitbashing project, combining a commercially available tank with supports made up from plastic sections.
Photo: Myles Munsey

Above
The restoration shed, seen in 2005 with a couple of diesels – a Barclay industrial and Drewry No.11249, along with a string of restored 'traditional' four-wheel wagons. A mix of old and new on a layout would be an effective contrast.
Photo: Steve Flint

Below
A Sudbury-bound Class 153 departs a damp Chappel site, passing the non-operational signal box. The extent of the museum's running line is evident in the distance, by the road bridge.
Photo: Myles Munsey

SUBSCRIBE
AND GET THE VERY BEST IN

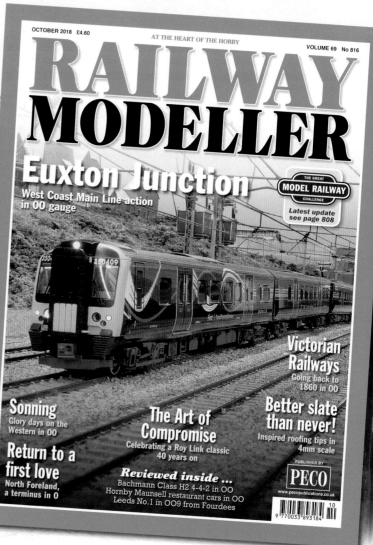
PLUS!

Chapter 4

Narrow gauge and miniature railways

It was narrow gauge railways that pioneered the concept of railway preservation in the UK during the 1950s, with the successes of the Talyllyn and Ffestiniog railway schemes paving the way for the hundreds of enterprises – of narrow and standard gauges – that flourished in the following decades.

The many narrow gauge preserved railways that we can enjoy today across Great Britain vary considerably in terms of their origins, size and operations. The revived Lynton & Barnstaple Railway, for instance, currently runs for barely a mile from the beautifully restored terminus at Woody Bay, which was originally a through station on the 19¼ mile line. However, despite its modest running line, there has been great efforts to restore the railway as close to its original condition as possible, with replicas of original L&B locomotives and painstakingly rebuilt rolling stock.

Above
The preserved Festiniog Railway, modelled in OO9 by David & Robert Waller. *Photo: Len Weal*

Below
Peter Leadley's *Cressington Light Railway* in OO9 is a supposed 21st Century 'tourist railway' on a former standard gauge trackbed. *Photo: Steve Flint*

By way of a contrast, the Bala Lake Railway in North Wales (see p100) was never originally a narrow gauge line at all; the route was in fact a standard gauge branch, the trackbed of which has been used to lay the 4½ miles of 2' gauge track. Passenger-carrying coaches are modern fabrications and train haulage is normally tasked to one of the railway's resident fleet of Quarry Hunslet 0-4-0STs.

It could be argued that the Bala Lake is not a preservation railway in the traditional sense, and that it is better categorised as a tourist railway. However, the surviving standard gauge structures and infrastructure that the BLR has restored, together with the use of the Quarry Hunslets (which have their own fascinating industrial histories) contribute to a rich preservation of railway heritage, albeit a mixed and highly unusual one.

From a modelling point of view, the prospect of running narrow gauge trains amid standard gauge infrastructure is a mouth watering prospect, as exemplified in OO9 by Richard Holder with his homage to the Launceston Steam Railway (see p88), which depicts the 2' system built along the route of the North Cornwall Railway.

The Brecon Mountain Railway treads a similar path to the BLR and LSR; utilising a former standard gauge trackbed that has been requisitioned for a narrow gauge

scheme, but this one using motive power obtained from overseas (see p18). Other examples of narrow gauge routes occupying former standard gauge trackbeds include the Gartell Light Railway near Templecombe in Dorset (formerly an Somerset & Dorset Joint Railway route) and the South Tynedale Railway (see p96).

Overseas locomotives and rolling stock

Utilising locomotives and rolling stock from overseas is, in fact, something that has been embraced wholeheartedly by the narrow gauge preservation movement. There are countless examples of items being imported to carve out a living on preserved lines in Great Britain, from the South African NGG16 Beyer-Garratts on the reborn Welsh Highland, to Austrian and Hungarian coaches on the (formerly freight only) Welshpool & Llanfair, whilst the Leighton Buzzard Railway is home to locomotives of Indian, South African, Portuguese and Spanish pedigrees. Such unlikely mixtures of outline can be achieved in model form by mixing, for example, British OO9 with overseas HOe items – there often being sufficient differences between items of narrow gauge stock from different countries to render the scale discrepancy (4mm vs 3.5mm) almost inconsequential.

Heritage credentials

Having made reference to narrow gauge preserved railways that occupy original trackbeds (whether these were originally of narrow or standard gauge), mention should also be made of schemes that have been developed on land that wasn't formerly of railway use. The Statfold Barn Railway in Staffordshire is a prime example; a privately-owned multi-gauge system that boasts an extensive and eclectic collection of preserved locomotives and rolling stock items. Furthermore, it is the provenance of the stock and artefacts that arguably gives the Statfold enterprise its heritage credentials, not the geographical location or the railway system itself.

Bressingham Steam Gardens is another example (referred to on p65), where narrow gauge and miniature railway systems have been developed on private land. Similarly, the 2' gauge Amerton Railway, which was developed adjacent to a working farm during the 1990s, is home to a selection of locomotives from builders including Bagnall, Kerr Stuart and Henschel (Germany).

It could even be argued that the Great Whipsnade

Railway – a 2'6" system around the grounds of the Bedfordshire wildlife park – can claim some heritage pedigree; despite it being operated as an attraction for visitors to the zoo, and not as a preservation scheme, the line boasts a stud of steam locomotives that formerly worked on the Bowaters Paper Railway, including a 1908-built Kerr Stuart 0-4-2ST (Works No.1049) and a 1920-built Kerr Stuart 0-6-2T (Works No.4034).

Tourist and miniature railways

Mention of the Great Whipsnade Railway does, however, bring us within the realms of tourist railways, which are schemes that exist without any 'preservation' credentials. Many miniature railways (which have a track gauge of 15" or less) can be categorised as tourist railways, and this includes the 7¼" gauge Beer Heights Light Railway at Pecorama, which was opened in 1975 using new locomotives and stock on former farmland.

The BHLR celebrated its 40th anniversary in 2015, which begs the question; has it created enough of its own history over those four decades to be considered within the wider

Top left
Fictional liveries, unusual combinations of stock and mixed gauge running lines are all hallmarks of the private Statfold Barn Railway. Here SBR No.9 *Jatibarang* (a German-built 2' gauge 0-4-4-0T Mallet that formerly operated in Indonesia) waits to cross *Saccharine* (a Fowler 2' gauge 0-4-2T from South Africa) at Oak Tree Halt.
Photo: Graham Lightfoot

Above
The Great Whipsnade Railway was constructed to take visitors on 'safari tours'. Although far removed from a heritage railway in the traditional sense, it does utilise locomotives of tremendous historical interest; pictured here is No.4 *Superior*, a 1920-built Kerr Stuart Baretto Class 0-6-2T (Works No.4034), which was built new for the former Bowaters Paper Railway in Sittingbourne Kent. It arrived at the Great Whipsnade Railway, together with three other locomotives from the Bowaters system in 1970.
Photo: Colour Rail

Left
An early preservation view (c.1968) of the 15" gauge Ravenglass & Eskdale Railway in Cumbria, with 0-8-2 No.3 *River Irt* pictured, a locomotive that was rebuilt from one constructed in 1894 by Sir Arthur Heywood.
Photo: Colour Rail

Above
A one-third full-size steam locomotive, No.8 *Hurricane*, on the 15" gauge Romney Hythe & Dymchurch Railway.
Photo: Dave Enefer

Right
A model based loosely on the 7¼" gauge Beer Heights Light Railway at Pecorama, built using proprietary OO mechanisms and track.

heritage railway movement alongside such pioneers as the Talyllyn or the Keighley & Worth Valley railways? That's up for debate, but certainly from a modelling point of view tourist railways often share the same anachronisms that can be found on heritage railways, with steam traction operating in a contemporary setting with modern structures and road vehicles. On this basis, a miniature tourist railway by Peter Leadley is presented in this chapter, contributing as it does to the overall theme of this volume.

Next steps

Narrow gauge heritage railways certainly have plenty to offer for the modeller, and indeed such schemes have historically been much more prevalent in the hobby than models of standard gauge preservation systems. Furthermore, the continuing growth of ready-to-run OO9 models from the likes of Peco, Bachmann and Heljan will only serve to strengthen the appeal of modelling narrow gauge subjects in the years to come.

A selection of narrow gauge and miniature railway schemes are presented in the following pages, but for further ideas relating to narrow gauge modelling, refer to our dedicated volume on the subject; *Your Guide to Modelling Narrow Gauge Railways* (ref.PM-203).

Launceston Steam Railway

In the tracks of the Atlantic Coast Express

Built in OO9 by Richard Holder

Some 50 or so years ago, an enthusiast by the name of Nigel Bowman bought a redundant industrial steam locomotive for the princely sum of £60. It was a small but significant part of his bold dream to build and run his own steam railway. The years passed until, in 1983, his dream became a reality, he and his wife Kay started operating their own line in Launceston along part of the standard gauge trackbed.

Richard regularly visited the Launceston Steam Railway, so when he was considering what he should build for his next OO9 exhibition layout, it was not a difficult decision. Once he had spoken to Nigel and Kay and explained what he was hoping to do, they were so welcoming and helpful. He was taken up the line on the footplate of Covertcoat at his next visit and given permission to photograph and measure structures and rolling stock.

Richard aimed to create a likeness that may not be accurate in every detail, but he hopes it is immediately recognisable to those who know Launceston station and the immediate surroundings. (The station canopy was built using an adapted Wills kit with supports from Langley Models.)

On all his previous layouts Richard built the baseboards from scratch using mainly plywood with softwood frames. For Launceston he obtained kits of baseboard parts produced by Model Railway Solutions of Poole, Dorset. Richard found the staff to be very helpful, whilst the parts were cut accurately and were easy to assemble. There are four 4' x 2' boards arranged in an L-shape.

Peco OO9 'main line' track and Peco points were used, some 'main line', but the majority being the live frog 12" radius types. SEEP point motors are powered from a Gaugemaster capacitor discharge unit. All point motors are wired to include a frog polarity switch so that there is no need to rely on the point blades to conduct current.

All of the rolling stock is fitted with Greenwich couplings with a loop at one end only. Automatic uncoupling is achieved by electromagnets, which were obtained from Gaugemaster, fitted below the baseboard.

The buildings were built using mainly card or foamboard with plastic or etched brass windows and doors. Richard used Redutex self-adhesive embossed sheets for a number of surfaces, including brick, stone, tiles, corrugated iron, etc. The sheets are quite expensive, but they are easy to use. They are all pre-coloured, reducing the painting required, although he weathered most of the surfaces.

The ground was built up using Celotex insulation material, used in the building trade. It is lightweight and very easy to cut with a kitchen knife, does not make the same mess as polystyrene, and can be stuck down with simple PVA glue. Ground cover was a mixture of static grass from Green Scene, and various scatter materials from a number of different manufacturers. Trees and bushes were mainly built from Woodland Scenics materials. Other greenery was obtained from the Polish manufacturer Polak.

More photos and videos of this layout and Richard's other exhibition layouts can be found at:
http://richardholder.org.uk/index.html

Above
All four of the LSR's Quarry Hunslets on shed (which is nicknamed 'Toad Hall'), from left *Covertcoat, Lilian, Velinheli* and *Dorothea*.

Left
The station site as seen from the A388 road bridge, under which pedestrians gain access to the site.

Right
Lilian emerges from under the Town Mills Street bridge with open-balcony coaches.

Left
Covertcoat and train ready for departure. The museum and café are in the distance. *All photos: Richard Holder*

Right
Dorothea trundles a couple of former Royal Naval Armaments Depot wagons near the station.

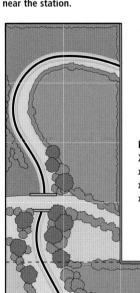

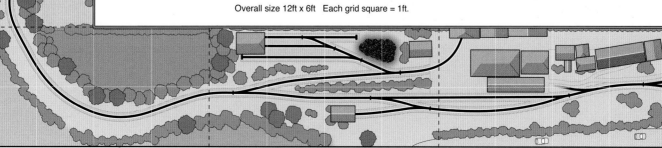

LAUNCESTON
Overall size 12ft x 6ft   Each grid square = 1ft.

Dduallt

The Ffestiniog Railway's spiral turn

Right
Driver's eye view of the railway looking from a Porthmadog-bound train. The bridge carries the railway on to Blaenau Ffestiniog.
Photo: Andrew Burnham

To Porthmadog

To Blaenau Ffestiniog

Woodlands

Barn

Lake

Rhoslyn

Up →

SC

← Down

Scenic dimensions: 9' 4".
Each grid square = 1ft x 1ft.

Left
Double Fairlie *Merddin Emrys* drifts downhill around the spiral towards the station and passes the distinctive fir tree. The first coach is crossing over the railway. The photo was taken in May 2011.
Photo: Andrew Burnham

Above
In model form, Blaenau-bound *Blanche* prepares to meet one of the Double Fairlies in Dduallt station. During the period depicted, the loop was not normally used to cross trains.
All layout photos: Len Weal/Peco Studio

Built in OO9 by David & Robert Waller

Modelling a real location is immensely challenging; especially when it depicts a tourist railway that is well known by the general public and enthusiasts alike (not forgetting the many volunteer 'Deviationists' who built the line in the first place!).

The model of Dduallt is nominally set in 1988/9 when the passing loop was still in situ, although not strictly timetabled for crossings and, furthermore, all the main line locomotives were in traffic. However David & Robert succumbed to the irresistible temptation to model beyond these set dates which explained the presence of Palmerston, Harlech Castle and the push-pull set, to name a few, on the layout.

The quality of construction of the trackbed on Dduallt was paramount to the finished layout's performance due to the gradient on the spiral. David & Robert spent many hours evaluating the performance of their locomotives on a gradient test rig (two metres of track on a length of 2" x 1" raised at one end – hardly high tech!) before committing to the final layout design. They had to establish what loads and train formations they expected each locomotive to haul and, having arrived at an acceptable gradient ratio, designed the height of Rhoslyn Bridge and the track plan of the layout around this imperative. Therefore Rhoslyn Bridge was actually set in a slight dip to maximise the height of the bridge and length of climb around the spiral.

Most of the spiral at Dduallt was built up on embankments or through cuttings, and as a consequence there is much exposed rock in the vicinity; either in the form of blasted rock faces or spoil that has yet to be engulfed fully by nature. The rockfaces on the model were created using real rocks, broken into suitable sizes with a large hammer, which were then pressed mosaic fashion into the wet Artex mixture and remained securely fastened. Merionethshire's finest road dressing chips made very realistic rock spoil, although real slate from the Dduallt area looked too dark for a realistic blasted face. Rocks from the more southerly Rhinog mountains sufficed instead. With the amount of rock supported within the scenery, adopting a heavyweight approach to baseboard construction was imperative.

The few buildings at Dduallt – Rhoslyn cottage, a barn, temporary toilet block and the signal cabin – were all scratchbuilt using Evergreen styrene strip and styrene sheet. The stiles and gates were also built on jigs using styrene strips.

All the locomotives are kits of varying parentage with some minor modification and improvements; heavily kitbashed in the case of Earl of Merioneth, Linda, Blanche and diesel Harlech Castle have had their chassis adapted with the addition of outside frames, and the Double Fairlies were built from Backwoods brass kits. The Welsh Highland's Russell also appeared, the superb chassis of which was built up from an old OO9 Society kit by Mick Moignard.

Dduallt was the builders' first attempt at OO9 modelling and also their first attempts at scratchbuilding, brass kits, working semaphores, chassis building and many other techniques. It therefore never ceased to amaze David and Robert that the layout should go on to receive the awards that it did during its time on the exhibition circuit. Their greatest satisfaction however, came when those who have worked on the Festiniog, particularly the Deviationists, passed comment on its resemblance to the real Dduallt.

Right
1979-built Fairlie 'reboot' *Earl of Merioneth* makes a cautious descent of the spiral. The real thing was withdrawn in 2018.

Bottom left
The two 'Penrhyn Ladies' on the FfR, *Linda* and *Blanche*, are seen double-heading a train for Blaenau Ffestiniog away from Dduallt and up the spiral.

Bottom right
Double Fairlie *Merddin Emrys* slows for the station stop at Dduallt, heading for Porthmadog.

The Clydach Railway

A fictitious North Wales preserved railway

Below
Pioneer Garratt K1 crosses the estuary on the ex-standard gauge section of the railway, heading for Aberclydach.
All photos: Richard Holder

Below
A Hunsley 2-6-2T at the modest facilities of Llanddarog – inspired by Tan-y-Bwlch on the Ffestiniog Railway, with its single island platform accessed by a footbridge.

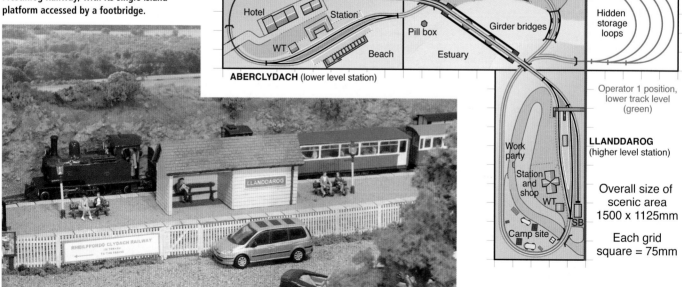

Operator 2 position, higher track level (red)

Backscene

Hotel

Station

Jetty

WT

Beach

Pill box

Girder bridges

Estuary

ABERCLYDACH (lower level station)

Hidden storage loops

Operator 1 position, lower track level (green)

LLANDDAROG (higher level station)

Work party

Station and shop

WT

SB

Camp site

Overall size of scenic area 1500 x 1125mm

Each grid square = 75mm

Above
General view of the Aberclydach station area, with a train pausing for custom. Spot the disused pillbox in the foreground, gradually being taken over by nature.

Below
The Garratt descends the gradient towards Aberclydach to meet a waiting train. Note the beach huts, which were made from cut-down Wills garden sheds, brightly painted.

Built in OO9 by Richard Holder

Richard built The Clydach Railway *as a fully portable scene, basing it on an imaginary slate-carrying enterprise which survived to be run by preservationists. He was keen to create a model that would appeal to a wider audience than just those who are interested in narrow gauge. At the outset, the features he sought to include were: a continuous circuit with at least two passing loops; gradients, so that trains could pass over and under each other; a simple track-plan with a minimum number of points to maximise reliability; varied scenery, which was to include a beach and an estuary; and curves of a minimum radius of 12". Also at least two trains operate independently and simultaneously, giving plenty of train movements to entertain the paying public at exhibitions.*

The supposed Aberclydach & Borthwynog Light Railway was created in 1896 and carried slate to the port of Aberclydach. But in autumn 1936, the market for slate collapsed. The railway struggled on through the war years but the carriage of passengers was unprofitable. The passenger service ceased in November 1946 and slate traffic also ended seven years later. The line was closed. However, inspired by the fledgling Talyllyn preservation movement, a similar effort was made: the Clydach Railway Preservation Society was formed, and took over the ownership of the railway in June 1954; it reopened at Easter 1955. During the 1960s the standard gauge branch line, which crossed the estuary on the substantial three-span girder bridge, closed: an ambitious plan was enacted to extend the railway, which eventually was opened in 1979.

By 1995 there were plans to extend the line even further, to create a 23-mile round-trip for tourists. This was a more ambitious plan than the earlier extension, yet by the summer of 2005, the final extension was completed.

The three scenic baseboards each measure 1500mm by 750mm. The board that carries the hidden loops measures 750mm by 750mm. Richard chose 9mm plywood for the baseboard tops and sides, which were cut for him by a local timber merchant. He cut the tops with a jig-saw to create the various levels. The cut edges were then glued and stapled to a card 'step'. This is surprisingly strong, as most of the card is curved, making it quite rigid.

Llanddarog – the higher level station – was inspired by Tan-y-Bwlch on the Ffestiniog Railway. It was in no way meant to be an exact replica, but those familiar with the Ffestiniog will recognise some similarities in the footbridge, car park, and shop, although they are in different positions to those at Tan-y-Bwlch.

The Clydach estuary occupies the central board. The cliffs were modelled using Sculptamold, and the water was formed using Artex, applied to the primed plywood surface, and shaped using a 1" paintbrush. This was then coloured using acrylic paints, and finally finished with several coats of high-gloss polyurethane varnish. The quayside walls were formed using Wills coarse stone sheets, with balsa to cover the joins. The harbour-side surface was built using Wills granite setts sheets.

Aberclydach is the lower level station. Woodland Scenics fine buff ballast represents the sand on the beach. Regular readers of RAILWAY MODELLER *will recognise the beach huts. They featured in Richard's Borth-y-Mawddach article. They were originally constructed using cut-down Wills garden sheds!*

Clee Valley Railway

A miniature tourist railway

Built in O9 by Peter Leadley

Having an interest in miniature railways by being involved with the 15" Cleethorpes Coast Light Railway, a layout in O9 – as the scale/gauge is normally referred to – started to take shape in Peter's mind. The period would be the early part of the 21st century, so items on the layout needed to reflect this particular era.

The baseboard construction comprises a 6mm top with supports from 44mm x 21mm PSE softwood with the long edges of each board stiffened with a 100mm piece of 9mm ply running the full length of each board. The legs were again made from 44mm by 21mm PSE softwood with the corner joins braced with a 6mm ply triangle plate.

The turntable is a Peco N gauge one operated by a simple mechanism which runs via gears to the back edge of the baseboard and terminates in a detachable handle. The over-riding aspect here was that the tracks were not parallel to the front edge of the baseboard but angled away from the edge through the proposed station platforms towards the turntable. So getting the turntable in the right place was paramount to the laying of the track. 1/16" cork was laid following the track plan and the track glued onto this.

The coaching stock was built from kits by Avalon and Finelines; some scratchbuilt ones from Colin Peake are also operated. The Avalon stock was fitted with bogies produced by Minimum Gauge Models. The bogies were fitted with wheels from Dundas Models. All the stock was fitted with B&B 3mm couplings as used on Peter's OO9 layouts.

The loco stock is currently as follows:

- Bonnie Dundee, an 0-4-0 tender loco built by Paul Windle using a Bull Ant motor bogie and modelled on the original from the Ravenglass & Eskdale Railway.
- Janette, a 2-4-2 tender loco built by Paul Windle using an old Farish 4-4-0 compound loco chassis; it was based on the Twining/Guest locos Siân and Katie.
- Sheila, an 0-4-4 based on the Muir-Hill i/c loco Pretender from the R&ER, on which it ran as a steam outline loco. It too was built by Paul Windle.
- Jacqui, a 2-6-2 based on Lydia from the Perrygrove Railway, although slightly underscale to suit its Life-Like chassis. Built by Paul Windle, this has been recognised by Perrygrove Railway members who saw it on the layout.
- Stella, an 0-6-0 freelance loco built from a Minimum Gauge Models kit by Ken Gibbons for Peter and running on a Farish N gauge Class 08 outside framed 0-6-0 chassis and has proved to be very reliable in operation.
- Charlotte, a 2-6-2T, started out in life as an OO9 Hunslet Welshpool & Llanfair loco, modified to allow the fitting of a 7mm scale driver.
- Effie, an 0-4-0 built from a kit from N-Drive Productions and based on the original Heywood design, tends to spend its life on a piece of track outside the museum on the layout. It does get the odd run, when Peter is asked if it works!
- A small diesel, as yet un-named; it is a 'Mite' kit running on a 0-6-0 Bachmann 'brick' chassis.

There is much to recommend modelling a modern tourist railway, and it makes a change from the run-of-the-mill Welsh quarry scenes and other industrial prototypes.

Above
Jacqui about to depart, standing beside the open-air ground frame. A dignitary has rolled up – perhaps to see plinthed *Effie* running!

Below
The driver of Bonnie Dundee eases his charge off the turntable release: this useful device allows turning and run-round in one movement.

Above
Trains have a mix of enclosed and open carriages, as it typical of railways of this nature. Tail lamps are still required...

Right
The engine shed is home to steam-outline i/c loco Sheila, being tended by workshop staff. Passing by is *Bonnie Dundee*.

Below left
A quick turnaround of locos is achieved by loco cassettes, which engage with the yard tracks via pins and tubes for alignment and transfer of current.

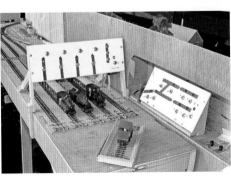

Operating area

Fiddle

Museum

Road

Station building

CLEE VALLEY RAILWAY
Scenic area: 10' 4" x 2'. Each grid square = 1 sq ft.

Alston station

PROTOTYPE FEATURE

The South Tynedale Railway

ALSTON TERMINUS

Carriage shed

Station building

Control panel

Signal cabin

Overall roof

Water tank

Crane

SOUTH TYNEDALE RAILWAY
Overall dimensions: 6' x 5'.
Each grid square = 1ft x 1ft.

Wagon shop

Trees act as scenic break

Locomotive works

Peninsula section provides a length of 'main line' run

Barn

Control panel

KIRKHAUGH STATION

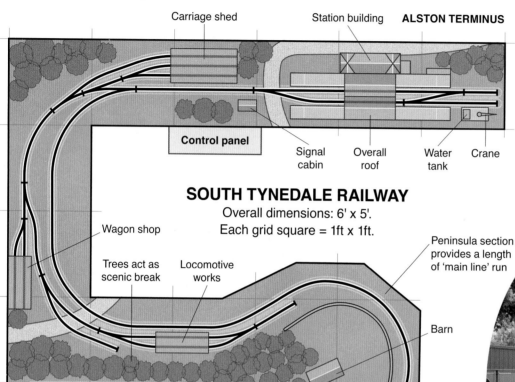

Above
Photographed at Alston in 2000, Henschel-built (in 1948) 0-4-0T Helen Kathryn is seen with a typical train. The loco has since been repainted blue.
Photos: Alan Pike or as credited

Below
Ex-NCB Hunslet diesel No.9 growls past the carriage sheds with an outbound service.
Photo: Dave Enefer

Below
Work under way to erect a new canopy and build a second platform at Alston in 2017.
Photo: Dave Enefer

Below
The original standard gauge train shed at Alston, with a J39 ready for the off.
Photo: Colour Rail

Above
Seen in 2000, the STR's then northern extremity was Kirkhaugh.

Left
Alston signal box was relocated from Ainderby, and oversees run-round movements.

Below
The original station building, seen from the road side.

Bottom
Peckett 0-6-0ST *Harrogate*, pictured here outside the modern style workshops at Alston, whilst on loan from the Statfold Barn Railway in June 2017.
Photo: Dave Enefer

The Railway described

Alston, the highest market town in England, nestles in a hollow in the hills which reach to a height of over 2000'. The uplands are bare and forbidding but the town is sheltered in the valley of the South Tyne river, the sides of which provide sheep pasture and woodland as a setting for the railway which has the valley almost to itself, for the A686 and A689 roads are mostly out of sight.

The Newcastle & Carlisle Railway promoted a branch from Haltwhistle to Nenthead which was authorised by an Act in 1846. Again the terrain won to some extent because an Act of 1849 allowed the line to be truncated at Alston.

The standard gauge branch, with earthworks for double track, opened on 17 November 1852 and provided the only reliable service for people and goods until 1976. The decline began after WW1 with the release of cheap army lorries and the arrival of more reliable buses. It was accelerated after WW2 for similar reasons to which was added the consequences of the spread of the private car.

The application for the closure of the line led to the requirement to provide an all-weather road including a new road bridge over the South Tyne at Lambley. When these works were completed, the line was closed in May 1976 and lifted soon after.

Strenuous efforts made to re-open the line by the South Tynedale Railway Preservation Society as a standard gauge operation failed but success has come with a 2' gauge line from Alston on the trackbed of the old branch which currently runs some five miles to Slaggyford; the intention is to reopen the route in full to Haltwhistle.

The site at Alston is a vestige of the old station area with, fortunately, the old station buildings. However, the loco shed has gone; the modern-day car park is on the site of it. The goods shed is in private hands but not apparently in use. The impressive signal box came from Ainderby on the Northallerton to Hawes branch. Alston station area is controlled by fully interlocked signalling.

The Society was fortunate to be able to use and adapt a commercial building near the station for the carriage works. A loco shed and works building and a large carriage shed have been constructed further down the line on the site of part of the former freight sidings.

In 2014, the railway was awarded a sizeable Heritage Lottery grant to expand and maintain the railway: the works involved the creation of a second platform at Alston, and the erection of an overall roof; solar panels have been installed to provide a green energy supply.

The plan is a reasonably accurate adaptation of the prototype with just a few alterations so as to fit the space as shown. One advantage of OO9 is that whilst layouts are not much narrower than 4mm standard gauge ones, they are generally shorter, enabling longer main line runs to be squeezed in. In this instance this has been achieved by using a peninsula section that doubles back on itself. A row of dense trees acts as a scenic break between the two scenes.

Of course, OO9 is very much a model maker's scale and the locos and rolling stock will all have to be sourced from kits and conversions. Track and points, as drawn, are available ready-to-lay in the Peco Streamline range.

(Abridged from an article by Alan Pike, published in RAILWAY MODELLER June 2009.)

The Lynton & Barnstaple Railway

PROTOTYPE FEATURE

Through Exmoor by rail

The Railway described

'Perchance it is not dead, but sleepeth' – the famous inscription on the wreath of bronze chrysanthemums which was laid at the buffer stops at Barnstaple Town station to mark the last day of operation of the Lynton & Barnstaple Railway, on Sunday 29 September 1936. It was sent by retired Royal Navy Paymaster Captain Thomas Woolf, who lived at Woody Bay: it is thus entirely appropriate that the reawakened L&B has its headquarters at the station which served the hamlet not far from Lynton. The station building, in its attractive Swiss Chalet style, was modelled in 2015 by Bachmann as part of its Scenecraft range of ready-to-plant resin structures (see p106), as part of the renaissance of ready-to-run narrow gauge equipment suitable for the L&B modeller in 4mm scale.

The present L&B runs from Woody Bay – at 964' above sea level the highest point on not only the line but the entire former Southern Railway system – south-westwards to a run-round loop at Killington Lane, a distance of approximately one mile. The loop is at road level here, and to the side of the original formation. The trackbed was covered over when the cutting to the bridge which carries the lane itself was filled in after closure; work is under way to clear the track bed and reveal the bridge once more.

Formed 40 years ago in 1979, the Lynton & Barnstaple Railway Association has made steady progress with its ambitious plan to reopen as much of the L&B as possible. Land and structures have been acquired, and the association recently won planning permission to extend its line from Killington Lane to Parracombe and beyond, to Blackmoor Gate and Whistlandpound Reservoir. The railway is fortunate to have four fully-restored coaches from the railway, with a fifth being returned to traffic. Woody Bay is home to the loco shed and workshops, although it is anticipated that these facilities will be supplanted by new buildings when the line reaches Blackmoor Gate. For full details about the railway, its volunteers and aspirations, visit: www.lynton-rail.co.uk

Modelling the L&B in OO9 took a great step forward in 2013 when Peco released its models of the four-wheel open wagons and vans, to be followed by several types of bogie coach, and the bogie opens. There was a further boost to the ready-to-run arena when Heljan released its models of the Manning Wardle 2-6-2T in 2017. Further rolling stock is under development, and Heljan announced its plans to model the Baldwin 2-4-2T Lyn at the Warley show in 2018. (To complement these locomotives, albeit in not prototypical fashion, Bachmann included a Southern green-liveried Baldwin 4-6-0T in its 2019 programme; a believable 'just supposing' model.)

Above
On 30 September 2018 – 82 years and one day after closure – replicas *Lyd* and *Lyn* storm up to Woody Bay.
Photo: Andrew Burnham

Below
Southern rail-built posts have lower quadrant arms. The Exmoor coast is just visible in the right distance.
All other photos: Tim Rayner

Below right

The locomotive shed and workshops occupy the trackbed at the Lynton end of the site. When the time comes to reawaken the section towards Lynton, these facilities will be removed.

Below

One of the railway's diesel locomotives is *Pilton*, a Drewry originally exported to Australia; it was modified and re-engined for use on the L&B, including work to allow it to conform with the railway's tight loading gauge. Named after the part of Barnstaple where the principal L&B works was situated, the loco wears pseudo Southern black livery.

Bottom

Three fully restored coaches make up an off-season train, photographed on 6 November 2018. The ground frame in the rebuilt signal box is locked before departure of trains, and opened when run-rounds need to take place.

Cattle creep

Large tree

Hedge

Ground frame

KILLINGTON LANE HALT

Shelter

Road to Killington village

Car park   **WOODY BAY STATION**   Station building   Signal cabin   Coal stage   Water pipe   Engine shed

LYNTON & BARNSTAPLE RAILWAY

Overall dimensions: 8' x 6'. Each grid square = 1ft x 1ft.

Llanuwchllyn station

PROTOTYPE FEATURE

The Bala Lake Railway

Below
Holy War prepares to return to Llanuwchllyn from the railway's current terminus, Bala Lake Halt.
Photo: Andrew Burnham

Right
The original goods shed, now surrounded by the shed and yard of the BLR. The signal box is also a surviving structure.

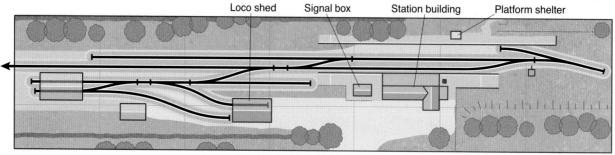

Loco shed   Signal box   Station building   Platform shelter

LLANUWCHLLYN STATION
Scenic length: 7' x 1' 6". Each grid square 1ft x 1ft.

The Railway described

The former Great Western route from Ruabon to Barmouth features two entirely separate preservation schemes; the Llangollen Railway is gradually being extended westwards with its new terminus at Corwen taking shape as this publication was in preparation (2019). The other railway is the 1'11⅝" gauge Bala Lake Railway.

The 54½-mile roue from Ruabon – on the Shrewsbury – Wrexham main line – to Cardigan Bay at Barmouth was constructed piecemeal by several local companies, all of which were taken into the Great Western 'family' by 1896. There were two routes branching off this east – west secondary line, running northwards; the London & North Western met the Ruabon – Barmouth line at Corwen, trains running between Rhyl and Corwen via Denbigh. The other branch left Bala Junction for Bala itself, before meandering up to an end-on intersection with another LNWR branch off its North Wales main line; the still-extant Llangollen Junction – Blaenau Ffestiniog segment of the national network. (The oval of routes thus created became famed in later years for the Land Cruise touring trains.)

The Ruabon – Barmouth line was slated for closure in January 1965; severe flood damage in the region mean that traffic was interrupted the previous month. Remarkably, services were resumed only a fortnight before they were withdrawn for good.

The westbound trek from the dip at Llangollen ran at a steadily rising gradient, with few level stretches, for about 30 miles before the route dipped downwards to the sea. The last station before the summit was Llanuwchllyn, around three miles east of the summit and 32 miles from Ruabon. The Bala Lake Railway – Rhielffordd Lyn Tegid – made the site its headquarters and began laying track on the former standard gauge trackbed (leased from Meirioneth County Council) in 1972. Flat-bottom rail was screwed to reclaimed sleepers, that were simply standard gauge ones cut in half. Trains began running to Glanllyn, the temporary terminus just over a mile to the east, on 13 August that year. Gradual extensions alongside its namesake lake brought the route to the eastern end, on the site of Bala Lake Halt by 1979. The railway offers a nine-mile round trip which occupies an hour amidst the breathtaking Welsh scenery. The railway's eastern terminus is a rather simple affair, but the town of Bala can be reached on foot in 10 – 15 minutes.

Moves are afoot to extend the railway into Bala itself: land has been acquired, funding raised and plans prepared: the Bala Lake Railway website has details of the trust that has been established to make this happen.

Visit: www.bala-lake-railway.co.uk

Top
0-4-0ST *Holy War* was built by Hunslet in 1902 and formerly worked at Dinorwic Quarry. Sister *Maid Marian* is also part of the Bala Lake fleet.

Above
This view eastwards shows the rest of the site. The modern window in the end wall of the former goods shed replaced the smaller-paned original.

Below
Evidence of the standard gauge origins of the station is clear to see in the platform spacing, something to bear in mind in a model.

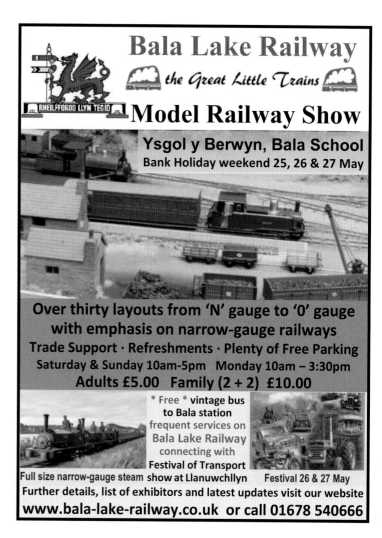

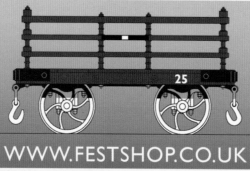
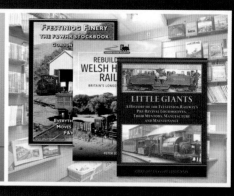

Chapter 5

Modelling the preservation scene

Modellers looking to recreate a heritage railway in miniature will find that they are well served with a multitude of suitable proprietary locomotive, rolling stock and structure models – particularly for OO and N gauges. The advantage of creating a preservation scene is the flexibility to mix structures and rail vehicles from different historical periods and geographical regions: an approach that will enable a huge selection of 'off the shelf' products to be utilised.

Locomotives and rolling stock

A cursory glance through the catalogues of the major R-T-R model railway manufacturers will reveal a large number of steam and diesel locomotive models representing specific preserved examples. This is hardly surprising however; where possible manufacturers will utilise full-size

Below
Oliver Reading made extensive use of 'off the shelf' stock on his *Sheaf Valley Railway* model (p42), mixing locos and rolling stock from different eras.
Photo: Derek Shore

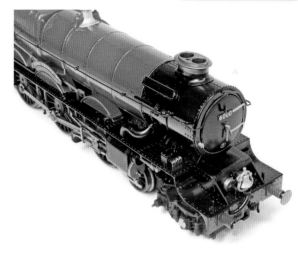

Above
The North Yorkshire Moors Railway's BR Standard 4MT 2-6-4T No.80135 in lined BR green, replete with modern yellow overhead warning flashes, as produced by Bachmann in OO.
Photo: Bachmann Europe Plc

Right
Models supplied with a high gloss finish make for ideal static museum exhibits, such as this version of No.6000 *King George V*, manufactured by Hornby for Locomotion Models.

Below right
Fox Transfers manufactures a wide range of locomotive headboards (etched in stainless steel), which can be fitted to models to replicate the seasonal special events staged by many preserved railways. The plates are available in 2mm, 4mm and 7mm scales.

Below
A selection of Bluebell motive power available ready-to-run in OO; Dapol B4 No.96 *Normandy*, Hornby Adams Radial No.488, Bachmann E4 No.B473 and Bachmann H2 Atlantic No.32424 *Beachy Head*.

vehicles to garner first-hand measurements and information for the development of new models, this approach having obvious benefits over relying solely upon published drawings and photographs.

Bachmann has a tradition of using preserved locomotives as the basis of Collectors' Club exclusive models, such as the OO version of Ivatt 2-6-2T No.41241 in Keighley & Worth Valley Railway lined red livery. However, preserved examples do also feature strongly in the firm's main OO range, including the North Yorkshire Moors Railway's BR Standard 4MT 2-6-4T No.80135 in BR lined green livery – a livery only carried by this member of the class during its preservation career.

Other preservation-specific models in OO include the Mid-Hants Railway's Stanier Class 5MT 4-6-0 No.45379 from Hornby, and the Bluebell's Adams B4 0-4-0T *Normandy* from Dapol. Furthermore, modellers looking to replicate part of the Bluebell Railway preservation scheme in 4mm will find that a surprisingly large number of the Sussex line's locomotive fleet have been produced ready-to-run over the years, including; E4 0-6-2T No.B473 (Bachmann), C Class No.592 (Bachmann), H Class No.263 (Hornby), P Class Nos.178 and 323 *Bluebell* (Hatton's), Adams Radial No.488 (Hornby and Oxford Rail), Dukedog No.9017 (Bachmann), Schools 4-4-0 No.928 *Stowe* (Hornby), Bulleid light Pacifics Nos.21C123 *Blackmoor Vale* and 34059 *Sir Archibald Sinclair* (Hornby), BR Standard Class 5 No.73082 *Camelot* (Bachmann), BR Standard Class 4 4-6-0 No.75027 (Bachmann), BR Standard Class 9F No.92240 (Bachmann) and BR Standard 4MT 2 6 4T No.80151 (Bachmann). And, for a forward-looking interpretation of the Bluebell, there is also the yet-to-be-completed replica

of H2 Atlantic No.32424 *Beachy Head* available from Bachmann.

It is also worth noting the series of exclusive models marketed by Locomotion Models under its National Collection In Miniature label; many of these have been released to mirror museum exhibits in the National Collection – even down to the gloss finish and polished metalwork, such as No.6000 *King George V* (Hornby).

Recent years have seen a proliferation in ready-to-run O gauge models, which has seen a number of preservation examples covered; Dapol, for instance, has produced models of the Fowler 3F 0-6-0T and GWR 57xx 0-6-0PT, which have been released in the guises of the Severn Valley Railway's Nos.47383 and 7714 respectively. The Fowler 3F was also the subject of a retailer exclusive version decked out as the Midland Railway Centre's preserved No.16410 (BR No.47327) in pseudo red livery.

Above
Preservation liveries are also available in O gauge; this Dapol Fowler 3F 0-6-0T in red was produced as a retailer exclusive.
Photo: DCC Supplies

Above right
The Bachmann (USA) 'Skarloey' model (nominally HO scale) can be transformed into a convincing replica of the Talyllyn Railway's 0-4-2ST, as demonstrated here.

Narrow gauge outline models in OO9 are also available for a number of preserved locomotives, such as the replica Lynton & Barnstaple 2-6-2T No.190 *Lyd* and 2-4-2T No.762 *Lyn* (Heljan) running on Festiniog and revived L&B railways respectively, together with the Bala Lake's 0-4-0ST Quarry Hunslets (Bachmann), the Leighton Buzzard's Baldwin WD 4-6-0T (Bachmann) – and even the Tallylyn Railway's No.1 *Talyllyn* and No.2 *Dolgoch*, which with some ingenuity can be created from the Bachmann (USA) models – nominally HO scale – of the Thomas The Tank Engine Characters for 'Skarloey' and 'Rheneas' respectively.

Structures and accessories

The opportunity for proprietary manufacturers to take first-hand reference from preservation sites has also extended to buildings and structures. The Hornby Skaledale and Bachmann Scenecraft (OO and N) ranges have featured numerous suites of 'ready-to-plant' resin buildings based on existing structures at preserved railways. Those based on the North Yorkshire Moors Railway's Goathland station (Skaledale) were used by Simon & Hannah Denham on their OO layout (see p30), whilst other examples include; Rothley (Great Central Railway, Bachmann – N and OO), Sheffield Park (Bluebell Railway, Bachmann – N), Highley (Severn Valley Railway, Bachmann – OO) and Woody Bay (Lynton & Barnstaple Railway, Bachmann – OO9).

Aside from proprietary items, there are also many kits available that are based around preserved structures, such as a laser-cut kit for Bridgnorth station building (Severn Valley Railway, Osborn's Models – 2mm), a GWR running shed (Didcot Railway Centre, Townstreet Models – 4mm) and the venerable plastic kit for Highley signal box (Severn Valley Railway, Ratio – 4mm).

Suitable scenic accessories, such as figures, road vehicles, signals and domestic buildings are all widely available. For those wishing to recreate the commercial services that many heritage schemes operate, such as 'Santa Specials', then etched headboards can be obtained from Fox Transfers.

Right
For some preserved stations, complete suites of ready-finished resin buildings can be obtained, which presents a distinct advantage to modellers who perhaps lack the confidence to build their own structures from kits or from scratch. Illustrated here are four items formerly produced by Bachmann Scenecraft – all based on examples at the preserved Shillingstone station, which is situated on the former Somerset & Dorset route.

Above
The Ratio plastic signal box kit (ref.500) that is based on the preserved example at Highley.
Photo: Jolyon Sargent

Right
'Ready to plant' from Bachmann Scenecraft for OO9 is this resin model of Woody Bay station. The Peco L&B coach provides scale.

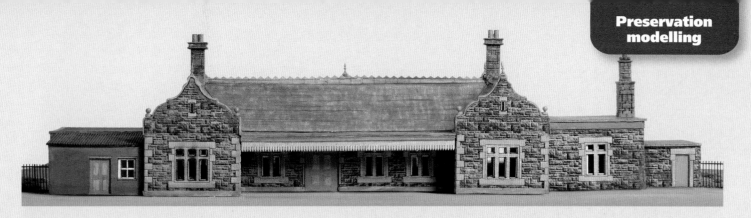

Above
Bridgnorth station building (Severn Valley Railway), produced as a laser-cut kit for N from the Bideford retailer/manufacturer Osborn's Models .

Right
The GWR built several new running sheds as 1930s Depression relief work under the Loan Act: the one at Didcot survives in preservation. The Townstreet model is a 4mm scale stonecast resin kit.
Photo: Townstreet

Below
Making a site visit presents an enjoyable means of collecting research material for a layout project based on an actual location in preservation. This is the terminus of the South Devon Railway at Buckfastleigh.

First-hand research

The aforementioned products that are available undoubtedly give a would-be builder of a preservation scheme a tremendous head start. However, the ability to visit a site and take your own first-hand reference is also a distinct advantage in situations where scratchbuilding the structures represents the only option. And what could be more appealing than a day out at a heritage railway where you can soak up the atmosphere of a bygone era, whilst taking photographs and measurements – all in the name of research?

Furthermore, the internet is a wonderful tool for researching preservation sites; track plans can be derived from satellite images (Google Earth for example), whilst there are plentiful photographs available – together with detailed stock lists and information – for most schemes.

Making a start

To all intents and purposes, the practical aspects of depicting a preservation scheme share much in common with layout projects based on historical themes, such as pre-nationalisation steam or BR blue TOPS diesels; certainly in terms of topics such as baseboard construction, track laying, train control and scenery. Therefore there is no need to retread this ground here – these topics are comprehensively covered in our other titles in the Peco Modellers' Library series, as outlined on p121.

Instead we present here a selection of step-by-step modelling projects that specifically relate to the theme of modelling the preservation era. All projects are demonstrated with OO examples, but the principles of each can be transferred just as easily to N, and even O, gauges.

Recreating a preservation-era workhorse in OO

s far as model locomotive lining projects go, the ornate GWR style livery scheme worn in recent years by the Dartmouth Steam Railway's brace of 42xx/'5205' 2-8-0Ts represents quite a challenge. Furthermore, the lining and names bestowed upon Nos.4277 *Hercules* and 5239 *Goliath* are historically unauthentic – ie, of the preservation-era – embellishments, meaning that dedicated GWR lining packs (available commercially for various other locomotive classes) aren't an option.

However, there are lining sheets available that can be adapted to suit: amongst the Fox Transfers range of waterslide transfers is a GWR lining pack intended for Collett 56xx/66xx 0-6-2Ts (ref. FRH4162); comparison of the two locomotive types will demonstrate that the dimensions of the sidetanks and bunker sides are sufficiently similar to enable this lining pack to be used on the 2-8-0T, albeit with some minor adjustments.

Several additional transfer sheets are also required to complete the transformation, all of which can be obtained from the same supplier; a generic GWR large tender locomotive lining pack (ref. FRH4150/1) to provide the lining panels for the cylinders and the single orange lining along the running plate valances, together with; ref.FRH4106/1 'Great Western' lettering, ref.FRH4108 GWR bufferbeam numerals and ref.FRH4150/NPL cabside numberplate lining. Perhaps surprisingly, suitable etched name and numberplates for No.4277 *Hercules* are readily available from 247 Developments.

Above
No.4277 *Hercules* climbs away from Goodrington with a service to Kingswear on 7 June 2016.
Photo: Joseph Connell

Right
A close up view of No.4277 *Hercules* showing one of its preservation-era nameplates. Note also the blanking plate on the smokebox (this particular locomotive having inside steampipes); a small detail that could be replicated on the model with some additional work.
Photo: Joseph Connell

Far right
A view of the completed model of No.4277, superimposed against a photo of the Torbay coast. The DSR often attaches a preserved Devon Belle Pullman Observation Car to its passenger services, which is represented here with a Hornby model.

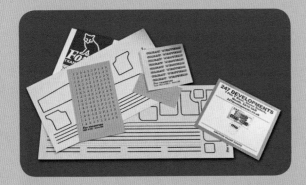

Top left

Suitable waterslide transfers were obtained from Fox Transfers, whilst etched name and cabside number plates were available to order from 247 Developments (www.247developments.co.uk).

Top right

The Hornby model of No.4283 in GWR green with 'shirtbutton' roundels (ref.R3123) provided a suitable starting point, it sporting inside steam pipes and parallel buffers as per No.4277.

Applying the waterslide transfers

The model should be first prepared for the application of the transfers as described in the accompanying step-by-step. Then, the lining can be applied in small stages (completing each side of the model separately), with each transfer first cut out from the rest of the sheet and immersed in warm water for 30 seconds or so. (Fox recommends adding a drop of washing-up liquid to the water.) Once the transfer has begun to separate from the backing sheet, it is then placed on the surface of the model, with a brush used to coax the transfer off of the backing paper and into its intended position. Final adjustments are made with the brush (adding more water if required) before dabbing away the excess moisture with tissue and leaving the transfer to dry.

All the lining on this model was positioned by eye, without recourse for guidelines or alignment marks, but others may prefer to use these. A set of good clear close-up prototype photos is invaluable (which for No.4277 can be sourced online), enabling the exact positions of the lining and lettering to be replicated; in certain situations the rivet detail on the model provides ideal datum points to work from.

Detailed user guides for applying waterslide transfers are available via the Fox Transfers website: **www.fox-transfers.co.uk**

CREATING No.4277 *HERCULES*

To prepare the model for applying the new lining and livery transfers, the original printed markings were first removed by repeatedly drawing a scalpel blade gently across the surface (right). The resultant witness patches prompted the repainting of the green parts of the body and bufferbeams; two coats of GWR green enamel were brush-painted, however spraying this on would have provided a superior finish. The photo (above left) shows the body after it had received a coat of gloss varnish (note how the cab glazing has been masked off). A coat of gloss varnish is recommended prior to applying the transfers and the shiny finish does in fact simulate quite nicely the polished preservation-era condition of the real No.4277.

2 To begin the process of lining the bunker was tackled first, cutting out one of the complete bunker lining panels from the Collett 0-6-2T set. Because the bunkers of the 2-8-0Ts are slightly longer, the top and bottom horizontal sections of the lining panel had to be removed. The remaining side portions were positioned as required (below), with longer replacement horizontal sections added at a later stage.

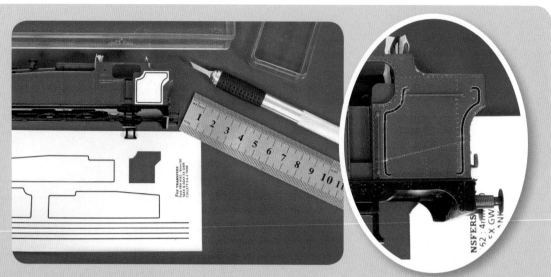

3 The main sidetank panel was added next, once again using a complete lining panel from the Collett 0-6-2T set. The sidetanks of the 2-8-0T are also slightly larger, meaning that this lining panel also had to be split into sections, positioned as illustrated.

4 The resultant gaps in the sidetank and bunker lining panels were then filled using the straight lengths supplied as part of the Collett 0-6-2T set, measured to allow for a very small overlap at each end and then coaxed into position (inset). Note how the transfer has been moved from the backing paper across to its intended location with the minimum amount of travel; this reduces the risk of the transfer becoming damaged or breaking up.

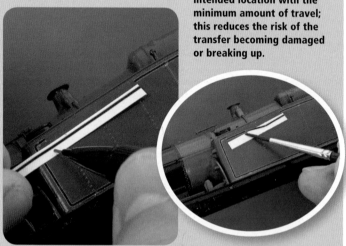

5 The boiler bands were added next, once again using the straight lengths supplied with the Collett 0-6-2T set. Each boiler band was formed of two parts, joined at the top.

6

Bufferbeam numerals were added next. These proved quite fiddly to apply because their positioning conflicted with the raised rivet detail. Small amounts of Humbrol Decalfix were brushed on to encourage the transfers to sit flush over the rivet heads.

7 The 'Great Western' lettering was applied in two parts, positioned in accordance with prototype photos of No.4277. The edge of a steel rule was used as a guide to ensure the lettering was set level. It is worth noting that the position and spacing of the lettering is unique to the DSR locomotives and differs to historical applications of 'Great Western' lettering on 42xx/'5205' 2-8-0Ts in plain green livery.

8 The single orange line that runs along the bottom edge of the running plate valance represented the trickiest stage of the lining process. Lengths of single orange lining are provided on the generic GWR large tender locomotive lining set. The lining was applied in sections measuring no more than 40mm in length; don't be tempted to apply the whole length of lining in one go! An approximation of the curves at each end of the valance were added using portions cut from the splasher lining panels, which are provided as part of the same sheet.

9 Cabside numberplates were fixed to the bunker sides, to which the numberplate lining panels were then added. It was found that the rebate around the inside edges of the etched plates helped to guide the transfers into the correct position, with little in the way of corrective adjustment required.

The last elements of the lining to be added were the rectangular panels on the cylinders. Suitable transfers were also provided on the generic GWR large tender locomotive sheet, but once again these needed modifying with additional horizontal fillets to replicate the unique DSR treatment applied to No.4277. After leaving the transfers to harden overnight, a light coat of gloss varnish was used to seal them in place and protect them from damage as a result of handling the model in the future. (Ordinarily a matt or satin finish is preferred by modellers, but gloss was used to retain the shiny finish as per the prototype.) The nameplates were then attached, using small cubes of styrene to mount them vertically – and set away from the smokebox – as is apparent in the photo on p108.

10

Volunteer accommodation from old coaches in OO

An omnipresent feature of many heritage railways is makeshift volunteer accommodation in the form of reconstituted passenger coaches, with vehicles either parked in sidings or on sections of track isolated from the main running lines. Such vehicles are usually found close to a railway's motive power base, the accommodation being particularly useful to members of the locomotive department; footplate turns often require an early start to raise steam, with volunteers electing to arrive on site the night before.

The actual coach types that can be found serving this purpose vary considerably, often coming down to what a railway has available to them. Former BR Mk.IIIa convertible sleeper vehicles are a particular favourite; these were ordered by BR in 1979 but became obselete soon after delivery owing to the cutting back of sleeper services by British Rail. Therefore, these presented a modern, readily-available means of providing sleeping accommodation for many preserved railways, including the Swanage and Bodmin & Wenford Railways. The advantage of using a rail-based vehicle over and above a 'bricks and mortar' structure is that, even if the coaches are destined to languish as static items on unconnected sections of track, the need for planning permission is conveniently negated.

Much use has also been made of older coach designs, such as GWR 'Toplight' and Hawksworth designs at Llangollen, whilst Bridgnorth is home to a rake of four BR Mk.I SKs – the latter sited on a disconnected section of track. However, from a modeller's point of view, almost any type of coach can be used to create such a cameo on a layout.

Volunteer accommodation in model form

When creating a model of volunteer accommodation, there are a number of common details that can be replicated: Foremost of these is the condition of the wheels and rails; being static for a long time causes the running surfaces to become heavily corroded, with trackwork itself becoming heavily overgrown. Much of the running gear on these vehicles is often not present, components sometimes being removed to maintain a railway's fleet of operational coaches; wheels are usually 'chocked' in any case. Similarly, gangway connections on corridor coaches are usually missing, with ends boarded up. Finally, there are usually staircases positioned for the volunteers to access the vehicles from ground level.

Many of these details are replicated on the model that forms the basis of the step-by-step feature presented here, for which a Bachmann coach has been used. It is presented in green and cream 'Camping Coach' livery, as a number of such vehicles at heritage railways have been adorned.

Top
The completed volunteer accommodation, set within a 'typical' preservation scene, complete with modern-style workshops, an unrestored locomotive (a Mainline BR Standard 4MT 4-6-0) and a shipping container used for parts storage.

Above
An ex-BR Mk.IIIa sleeper parked on an isolated section of track near the locomotive shed at Swanage. Note the green paint scheme and end staircase.

Right

The basis of this project is this Bachmann model, which was commissioned by Frizinghall Models & Railways (ref.34-251W), and finished in green and cream camping coach livery and based on the manufacturer's 57' LMS composite coach. However, all sorts of different coach models could be used as the basis of such a project.

CREATING A SLEEPING COACH FOR VOLUNTEERS

1 The model was dismantled and the first task was to remove the gangway connections. (These are often removed on coaches used for volunteer accomodation, with the resultant doorways blanked off.) The rubber gangways were popped out and sections of styrene sheet attached to the insides of the ends. The representations of the coupling hooks on the headstocks were also removed at this stage.

2

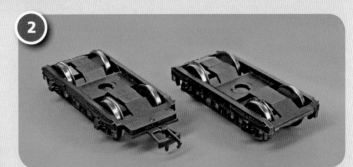

Because the vehicle was going to be a static item, the tension-lock couplings and bosses on the bogies were redundant. The bogie on the left is original, the one on the right has had its coupling and boss removed.

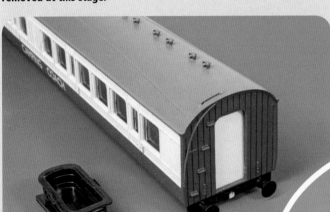

3

To depict a vehicle that had had its vacuum braking equipment removed, the relevant items were unclipped from the underside of the chassis, as illustrated.

4

The coach interior as supplied represented that of the standard LMS 57' composite, but coaches are often subject to significant alterations internally to create the necessary sleeping accommodation. Rather than build a new interior from scratch (which could be an interesting modelling project in its own right), sections of styrene were used to blank off some of the corridor doors and windows to give the impression of a modified interior.

5

With the coach reassembled, the wheelsets were painted black with Humbrol acrylic (ref.RC 401). Coaches used for volunteer accommodation have often been static for lengthy periods of time and therefore the running surfaces (particularly the tyre treads) would acquire a patina of rust. The treads on the model were painted accordingly, as illustrated.

Vehicle bodies tend to be kept in good external condition but the chassis, roof and ends were treated to a light dusting of Humbrol weathering powders.

A section of track alongside a station platform was chosen to locate the model. It was given the appearance of being seldom used by liberally covering the track with static grass and painting the surfaces of the rails a rusty colour.

Above

Stanier 5MT 4-6-0 No.44806 approaches Llangollen station with a service from Carrog. The vehicles on the higher level are all static coaches used as volunteer accommodation (including a former Hawksworth brake and Mk.I sleeper), situated alongside the railway's locomotive shed and workshops.

Wheel chocks were fabricated from triangular sections of styrene and fixed to the rails with cyanoacrylate. This was done with the coach *in situ*, but care was taken to ensure the wheels were not inadvertently glued to the chocks (so that the model can be removed from the layout if it is a portable system).

9

A staircase was created using modified parts from the Ratio accessory kit for a wooden staircase (ref.142). It was halved in length and the steps were reduced in width slightly. Stairways like these usually have a banister on one side only (to allow for the opening of the door). Styrene section was used to create a set of rear supporting legs, as illustrated.

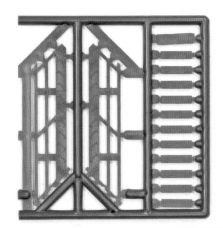
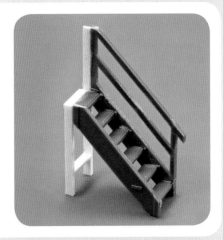

10

The finished model, surrounded by other items that are typical of yards at preservation sites, including the recovered shipping container, often employed by heritage groups as a means of storing tools or components.

Below
A feature of Bridgnorth station on the Severn Valley Railway for many years has been a row of four BR Mk.I SK coaches, which are parked on an isolated section of track behind Platform 1. Used as sleeping accommodation for footplate crews, they have been painted in BR Southern Region green livery.

Modelling an unrestored steam locomotive in OO

The contribution that the South Wales scrapyard of Dai Woodham made to Great Britain's standard gauge preservation movement was mentioned earlier in this book; hundreds of ex-BR steam locomotives were spared the cutter's torch, instead being sold by the scrapyard to preservationists between the late 1960s and early 1990s.

Whilst some early escapees from the yard were found to be in relatively good condition (such as No.43924, which was recovered from the yard in 1968 bound for the Keighley & Worth Valley Railway), the majority deteriorated significantly through years – sometimes decades – of exposure to Barry Island's salty sea air. Locomotives that languished in the yard into the 1980s became little more than rusted hulks, devoid of components and fittings.

It is testament to the will and determination of preservationists that more than 150 of these former residents of Woodham's scrapyard have been restored to working order. However, there are many unrestored locomotives awaiting their turn, examples of which can be found at many preserved lines and heritage railway centres.

If you are modelling the preservation era, then an unrestored locomotive represents an ideal project, which can occupy a siding, headshunt or bay platform.

The subject of this step-by-step feature is a OO gauge Hornby rebuilt Bulleid light Pacific. Some modellers may

question the cannibalising of what (in this instance) appears to be a 'perfectly good' model, but it should be noted that this example was purchased as a non-runner, and at a price that modellers would currently expect to pay for a new 4mm scale R-T-R carriage or similar item of rolling stock. This project is particularly suited to OO gauge, the second-hand market offering plentiful opportunities to acquire suitable donor locomotives. Alternatively perhaps, older models that are no longer used can be taken out of exile from the back of the stock cupboard and given a new 'lease of life' as a cameo of an unrestored locomotive.

Top
The completed model that forms the subject of this project – a rebuilt Bulleid light Pacific (Hornby) – is set within a scene redolent of the preservation era, as it awaits its turn for restoration from this rusting hulk to working condition.

MODELLING AN UNRESTORED LOCOMOTIVE

A Hornby rebuilt light Pacific model was obtained at an exhibition as a suitable candidate for modification, and despite being a non-runner was otherwise complete and in 'as new' condition. The model was finished as No.34008 *Padstow,* which wasn't actually one of the many Bulleid Pacifics that found their way to Woodham's. (Suitable transfers could be used to renumber locomotives accordingly, if desired.)

Locomotives very rarely arrived at scrapyards with name and number plates. They were either 'removed' by souvenir-hunting enthusiasts or taken off by running shed staff for safekeeping and sale through official channels. The moulded front numberplate on the Hornby model was gradually cut away with a knife. This task needed to be done carefully to avoid damaging the surrounding smokebox door detail. The door dart and nameplates were also removed at this stage to echo the condition of many unrestored locomotives seen in prototype photographs.

Locomotives that were towed by rail to private scrapyards such as Woodham's often had their connecting rods removed. Therefore the model was similarly treated. The front parts of the connecting rods on the model appeared to be riveted to the back of the crossheads and therefore, rather than dismantling the motion to remove the rods, they were just cut through with snippers behind the joints. More of the motion was then removed, including the coupling rods, eccentric rods and return cranks, to mirror the condition of many locomotives at Woodham's.

Left
BR Standard 4MT 2-6-4T No.80150 was still ostensibly in 'ex-Barry' condition when it arrived at Alresford on the Mid-Hants Railway in 2011. Devoid of many fittings, its restoration to working condition will be a substantial undertaking.

Below
A 1964 view of Woodham's scrapyard, with a trio of Bulleid Pacifics visible. Nos.34016 *Bodmin* (nearest) and 34028 *Eddystone* (centre) have both operated in preservation.
Photo: Rail Photoprints

4 Painting commenced prior to fixing the accessory details to limit potential damage whilst handling the model. Wheels, motion and buffer heads were coated with a black permanent marker to eliminate the factory shine of these parts. All black parts of the locomotive were given a metallic oily sheen by applying a thinned mix of enamel paints, using Humbrol No.53 Grey, darkened with Humbrol Black.

5

To give the locomotive a rusty appearance, the model was first dry brushed with a dark rust colour (Humbrol No.160 enamel paint). Smaller areas of 'fresh' rust were then applied (Humbrol No.100 enamel paint).

6

The whole locomotive was subjected to a similar weathering process. This view illustrates the patches of bright rust on the pipework below the cab and (particularly) the ashpan detail. The cabside numerals were made to look faded – by the sun and sea air – by applying tiny amounts of light cream acrylic paint.

7

This view illustrates the front end of the locomotive after fixing of the various accessory details provided by Hornby. Some parts (door straps, lamp brackets, door boss and buffer heads) have been picked out in white paint to mimic the treatment many locomotives in Woodham's yard received from preservationists eager to make their new purchases as presentable as possible cosmetically. The centre parts of the buffer heads were then given an oily black colour, followed by a covering of gloss varnish to simulate grease.

Above
There is plenty of potential for unrestored locomotive cameos beyond those that escaped Woodham's scrapyard. This Peckett 0-6-0ST (Works No.1567 Acton Hall No.3, built 1923) is pictured at the Foxfield Railway prior to its restoration commencing. *Photo: Phil Barnes*

8

Finishing touches to the locomotive included painting the brake rigging and drain cocks to match the rest of the locomotive. Sparing amounts of gloss varnish were applied to parts of the motion and lubricators on the running plate to give an oily finish.

Top
Stored locomotives awaiting restoration are often treated to rudimentary cosmetic work, partly to prevent further deterioration. Such is the case with ex-GWR large Prairie No.4110, pictured here at Minehead.

Above
Shades of rust! The shell of Fowler 4F No.44123, recorded at Bitton on the Avon Valley Railway, would make for an interesting exercise in painting and weathering.

9

The completed model. The tender was dispensed with to reinforce the fact that the model represents an unrestored, non-operational locomotive. Furthermore, many such projects seen at preservation sites are without tenders, these often having to be fabricated from scratch by the respective restoration groups.

Adapting a coach for propelling moves in OO

There are several examples of preserved lines and heritage railway centres that incorporate propelling moves as part of their passenger train operations, including the Ribble Steam Railway (see p76) and the Buckinghamshire Railway Centre (see p65). The need for trains to be hauled in one direction and then propelled back is due to a lack of run-round facilities at one or both ends of the running lines.

These propelling moves (see photo and caption above right) are distinct from trains that run 'auto-fitted'. Propelling moves make use of ordinary passenger coaches (such as ex-BR Mk.I brake vehicles) that have been adapted to enable them to be operated in this manner.

From a modelling point of view, adapting a brake coach to replicate

Above
A train arriving into Carrog station on the Llangollen Railway, having been propelled from Corwen. A second driver is rostered for these moves, who stands in the gangway with a view of the line ahead; he communicates with the locomotive driver via two way radio, calling out all signals, crossings and any other hazards. For emergency purposes, the second driver also has a vacuum brake gauge and a guards brake valve. *Photo: Martyn Moss*

these propelling moves is very straightforward, requiring just a suitable gangway cover to be fabricated, with only minor modification required to the model.

MODIFYING A BACHMANN Mk.I BSO FOR PROPELLING OPERATION

1 The gangway at the brake end was unclipped, with the end door then removed by chain-drilling around the edge using a mini-drill, cutting the waste away with side cutters. A figure was added inside the gangway to represent the second train driver. The tension-lock coupling was also removed from this end.

2 The gangway provided a template to mark out the cover plate on 10thou styrene sheet, with the window aperture marked out with reference to photographs. Holes were drilled to accept the wiper and vacuum pipe. The cover plate was then secured to the gangway with Plastic Weld.

3 The cover plate was painted with yellow enamel prior to adding the glazing (secured from the back) and wiper blade (a section of brass wire). The electric light cluster was formed of Modelu lamp lenses on a small rectangle of black styrene. The extended vacuum pipe was fashioned from the couplings supplied with the model.

4 In a scene redolent of an embryonic preservation project, the completed coach is propelled by a Hunslet 0-6-0ST (Hornby). Working LED lighting could be fitted if desired.

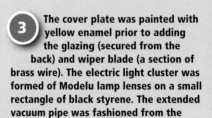

Acknowledgements

This publication would not have been possible without the input of the following:

Robin Brogden, Gordon Crapper, Simon & Hannah Denham, Richard Holder, Matthew Jackson, Peter Leadley, Nick Lloyd, Tony Peart, Trevor Powell, Oliver Reading, Peter Smith, David & Robert Waller, members of Warley MRC, Matt Wickham.

Bibliography & Further Reading

Your Guide to Railway Modelling & Layout Construction
Peco Publications, ref.PM-200
– second edition published in 2015
ISBN 978-0900586 00 2

2018 Peco Catalogue
Includes all the Peco Group products, incorporating Parkside kits

The Peco Modellers' Library Guide to Modelling Narrow Gauge Railways
Peco Publications, ref.PM-203
published in 2015
ISBN 0 9000586 03 3

The Peco Modellers' Library Guide to N Gauge Railway Modelling
Peco Publications, ref.PM-204
published in 2016
ISBN 0 9000586 04 0

The Peco Modellers' Library Guide to OO Gauge Railway Modelling
Peco Publications, ref.PM-206
published in 2017
ISBN 0 9000586 06 4

The Peco Modellers' Library Guide to O Gauge Railway Modelling
Peco Publications, ref.PM-208
published in 2018
ISBN 978-0-9000586-57-6

Peco 'Shows You How' booklets:
SYH2 Building Baseboards
SYH3 Laying the Track
SYH4 Wiring the Layout – part 1, first steps (revised edition September 2016)
SYH13 Modelling the Landscape
SYH17 Introducing DCC

Other publications/websites
Heritage railway websites (such as those listed in the RAILWAY MODELLER *On The Rails* guide to railway attractions, free with the June issue each year)

Back issues of prototype-orientated railway magazines such as *Railway World*, *Railway Magazine* and *Steam Railway* amongst others, which have accounts of preservation schemes from the 1950s onwards. Find second-hand copies at model railway exhibitions and heritage railway bookstalls.

Railway Adventure by L T C Rolt
2010 edition published by
The History Press,
ISBN 9780752455785

Barry – the history of the yard and its locomotives by Peter Brabham
published by Oxford Publishing Co in 2013 (now a Crécy Publications imprint)
ISBN 978-0-86093-643-5

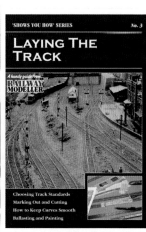

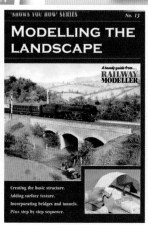

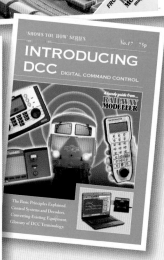

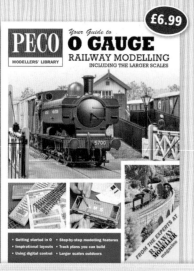

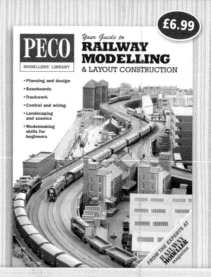
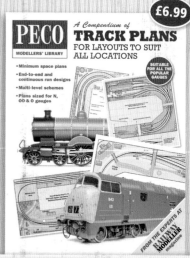
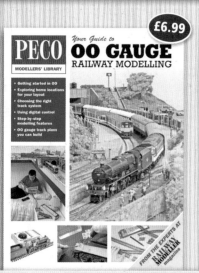
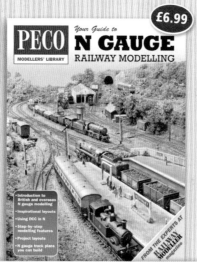
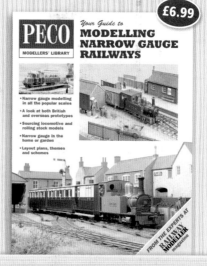

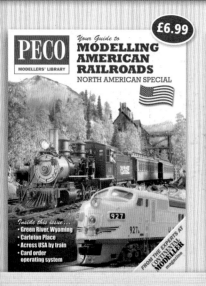

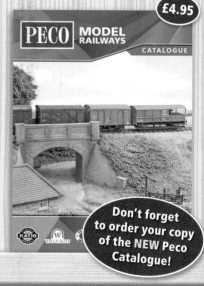